Start Selling Smart!

What really happens in a sales situation

and how to use it to your advantage.

This publication is designed to provide information with regard to the subject matter covered. It is sold with the understanding that this book is not intended to render specialized, legal, accounting, or other advice, for which the services of a competent professional should be sought.

No part of this book may be reproduced or utilized in any form or by any means, electronic or mechanical, including photocopying, recording, or by any information storage and retrieval system, except in the case of brief quotations embodied in critical articles or reviews, without permission in writing from the publisher.

Start Selling Smart!

All rights reserved.

Printed in the United States of America

Published by *Golden Leaf Press*

Copyright © 2009 Stuart J. Kamille

TO THE READER

This book is the result of 35 years of making mistakes and paying for them with lost opportunities. Fortunately for me, my partners, employees and my customers, were very forgiving and helpful. So over time I learned the craft of selling. It isn't the easiest of occupations.

If you've picked up this book hoping to find a way to improve the way you go about selling in your business career, I think you made a good choice. I hope you will find it a rewarding approach to making more sales, more profitable relationships and having more fun while doing it.

Knowing how to read your customer is a skill you can develop with time. Most salespeople learn it by bumping into situations time and time again, until it begins to dawn on them that every time you think you have the sale, something seems to happen and it just vanishes. At first, you're puzzled. What could have gone wrong? Then after a few more missed sales, you start to put two and two together and a little doubt appears.

Perhaps, you think, (rather uncomfortably), to yourself you're overlooking something. Somehow, the customer isn't reacting the way they should. Is it something that you're doing wrong? You know your material. You thought you answered all their questions. But for some reason, the customer just slipped through your fingers. What is wrong?

Slowly, (very slowly), and painfully, (very painfully), you notice that every time you lose a sale you keep hearing the same words and seeing the same things happen.

'THAT'S IT!"

You say to yourself.

"It must be something wrong with the client."

At least that's what I thought. It took me a few more years to realize that it wasn't the client…it was me. And it was so simple that I just couldn't see it. It was right there all along. There was nothing wrong with my presentation and there was nothing wrong with the client.

What I was saying and what they were saying were not matching up. I wasn't listening to what the client was actually saying. I was just hearing what they said and that isn't the same thing as understanding what they mean.

It's about communication. Communicating with your client means understanding what they mean, even if it's not exactly what they are saying. If you can discover the hidden meaning behind their words, you can be much more successful in closing a sale.

Did you ever wonder why it is that some salesmen make sale after sale and some starve? The answer is very simple. Good salesmen know their customer. They know how to read what they are saying. They understand them. This takes time. If you're not naturally gifted with that insight, then you learn this slowly after a great many sales calls. Finally, someday you learn that your customer is an open book. You just have to know how to read them.

That's where this book can really help. You can take the short cut this book provides and skip the bumps, bruises and hard knocks that otherwise will be required. Reading your client is a lot more than making lots of sales calls and getting to know them personally. Frankly, the difference between a good salesman and a mediocre one is simply experience. That experience helps a good salesperson take a potentially difficult situation and turn it around. It allows the salesperson to help the client see things in a way that is both good for his company, but also good for himself. This is not as simple as it might seem.

I don't do my own income tax anymore because I can't. I don't have the experience that my accountant does. I wouldn't presume to fly a jet aircraft or replace my car's transmission. I'm willing to go to someone else because they have lots of experience. Their experience, the fact that they've done the same thing dozens, hundreds maybe thousands of times, gives them a big edge.

If you're new to sales, you know that there are others out there who have more experience than you do. So the smart way to learn how to sell better is to go to them and ask.

They probably won't tell you much however, since they don't want you to take their sales away from them. That's where this book can help. I don't sell anymore. But I did it very successfully for a number of years. I always managed to close the sale. I always managed to get in the door and get to the right person and get the contract.

A lot of that was through sheer perseverance I admit. But once you are in the door and with the right person, it is what you do next that makes the difference between getting the sale and not getting the sale. That difference is simple.

It's knowing how to read what your client is thinking as you talk with them. It's as simple as mind reading. If you think mind reading is impossible I can assure you that it's not. At least mind reading is not impossible when you're discussing your product and their possible purchase of it.

The key is being aware of what your client is saying and doing as you talk. It's simply keeping your eyes and ears open and knowing what to look and listen for.

Observing these little things is smart. It gives you an edge which probably will keep you way ahead of your competition and help you react to what your client is thinking before they even realize it. It puts you in the position of always having the right answer at the right time. It makes you look good, it makes your product look good and it makes your company look good. All this adds up to a sale.

If I had to put a name to it, the best I could do, would be to call it "Smart Selling". Smart Selling has little to do with how smart you are. As a matter of fact much of Smart Selling has very little to do with what you sell or how you present or even what kind of salesperson you are. Smart Selling has a different focus. It's all about how the client feels. It's about the way they feel about you, your product, and the company you work for. It's probably quite different from what you would consider traditional selling.

There's a traditional view of selling and then there's Smart Selling. I imagine you will find that Smart Selling differs with just about every concept you thought would apply to making a sale. In some cases, it might actually be just the opposite of what you currently think.

If you've been selling for any length of time at all, you know selling is tough. It's disappointing and it's frustrating. Selling is not for everyone. Pressuring your client into a sale takes a lot of effort. It's the tough way to go about it.

Part of the problem with classical selling is the tools you are forced to use. Traditional selling tools are things like flip charts, canned presentations, snazzy brochures etc. They are designed to MAKE a sale.

It's rather like building a house. You start with the foundation and build up an overwhelming logical framework. Your customer would have to be an idiot not to realize the force of your argument. Such tools force you to treat your customer as if they know very little. But worse than that, they are aimed at making your customer agree. The tools are blunt, coarse and heavy handed. It's a LOT of work.

Smart Selling gives you another way to get the sale but without all that perspiration. The tools are quiet and unassuming but I've found them very effective.

The nice part about the technique is that it's applicable to anyone who has a product or an idea to sell. You don't have to be a sales person, you don't have to be a rep, and you don't have to be selling for a living. You can apply the same tools to any situation where you want your view to prevail. So if you're selling a cyclotron or a kiddy car or if you just want your boss to give you a raise, you can apply Smart Selling and get results.

You should be able to apply these tools and observations immediately. You won't have to memorize any scripts or remember any special sequence of steps or any of that. Smart Selling is Simple.

The whole idea behind Smart Selling is a focus on the customer. They are the important center of the activity and for that reason Smart Selling will work every time. So that's what you will find in this book. It's my experience (summed up in a few chapters) that I hope will enable you to make many of the sales that you might otherwise lose.

I've tried to make the text clear, entertaining and useful. I want you to get something out of this book and I want you to be glad you've read it.

If I've succeeded I'd like to know. If I haven't I'd like to know that too. Maybe there's a way I can make it better. If so, let me know. Send me an email at Skamille@Stuartjkamille.com, I'll be glad to hear from you.

SJK

CHAPTER 1
SELLING ISN'T WHAT YOU THINK

You can sell better. You can close more sales. You can get more repeat business. And you can do it just by watching and listening. But you have to know WHAT to look for and WHAT to listen for. That requires that you learn how to Start Selling Smart.

Reading your customer is based on the idea that buying is emotional. As a matter of fact, contrary to what most sales people imagine, I think all our decisions are determined more by the way we feel than the way we think. We might use logic and reason to determine the accuracy of certain things, but all the logic in the world isn't going to make a client buy something they don't feel comfortable with. That comfort level can distort any amount of logic.

In other words...if you client doesn't feel good about your product, you aren't going to argue him into buying it. He or she has to want it and the more expensive it is, the more they have to want it. So all selling is in the clients' mind. It's a question of feeling. Selling is emotional.

Here's a simple example. There's a hole on a golf course that I frequently play that has a steep ravine about 60 yards from the tee. I know I can easily hit a golf ball over that ravine, but just the idea of that ravine makes it a heart thumper every time I play it. Logically, I know I can easily hit over it. But emotionally, that drop-off looks mighty deep. And on that particular hole I often miss strike the ball and it ends up at the bottom of the ravine. It's an easy shot but try telling that to my golf ball.

The advertising business uses emotional appeals all the time to influence a purchasing decision and there is rarely much logic to it. We see it all the time.

Have you seen those ads for the watch that is guaranteed to withstand the pressure of the sea down to 900 feet or so? Isn't that about where submarines start to break up?

It's a pretty expensive watch. It does lots of other things to. It can act like a stopwatch and divide time down to fractions of a second. It tells the date and never needs winding and downloads the exact time every day. Now those are nice features. But logically how often do you need to know the date and the time to the split second while swimming at 900 feet beneath the sea? At that depth I imagine you would have exploded before the watch would, but is that really a good, logical reason to pay so much? Probably not. Yet even though there is no logical reason, lots of people will. It feels like it's worth the extra money. And because of the way they feel, they will buy it.

Every purchase has an emotional charge tied to it. Even pretty insignificant purchases are still governed by what "feels" right. If the client doesn't feel good about the purchase, that purchase isn't going to be made. Period.

Considering how important the way a client feels is to the decision to buy your product, you'd think sales people would spend a lot of time learning about it; trying to understand how to make the customer feel right. But they don't.

Most sales people think selling is about their product and about their presentation. They believe that if they study their presentation and practice and practice to get their presentation perfect, they will close the sale. They think the perfect presentation will sell the product.

Well, I don't believe the presentation sells the product. No one buys because of a presentation. Your customer must feel that they want, or better yet, need the product.

It's the way the customer feels that determines the sale. So in some way you have to present the product so your client will feel that the product is right for them. It's your job to help them feel satisfied with the purchase.

In a way it takes you off the hook. It means the salesman isn't responsible for making the sale. The salesman is responsible for making the buyer responsible for the sale. That is, it's the buyer who decides to buy because of the way the salesman helps them feel about their product.

To put it another way,

SMART SELLING

SALESMEN DON'T SELL...BUYER'S BUY

But how do you do that? How do you learn to understand the way your customer feels so that you can position your product and strike just the right tone?

You have to read the way the client feels. You have to see your product through their eyes and understand their feelings. Then you can determine what the client wants and can point out something about the product that will fill that desire. Approaching the sale in this way makes the sale a lot easier because there is no pressure to it. The salesperson is helping the client see the product in a particular way or reassuring the client that the product will perform in a particular way.

If you agree on the importance of the emotional element in sales then it becomes obvious that rehearsing and rehearsing your presentation isn't going to be very helpful in making a sale. A good salesman must study his client not his presentation. That gives the salesperson insight into his customer. Insight requires observation and information. Fortunately there's a lot of information available. It's the observation that is generally lacking.

Paying close attention to how your customer reacts to what you say and to what comments they make in response to what you say, allows you to understand the emotional issues that make up a customer's attitude toward your product. You'll be pleased to know that this isn't very complex. It doesn't require you to memorize a series of answers for various situations. You won't have to fill your head up with various scripts or terminology. You won't have to learn when to ask for the order or the right time to close. That's because it's based on the client's emotional temperature not on your delivery and that is going to make this easy. When the client is ready, you make the sale. But you have to realize that the only time that is going to happen is when they feel right about it and not one second sooner.

Traditionally the act of selling has undergone a lot of analysis. It's not surprising; everyone who sells for a living wants to sell better. And the most straightforward way to approach the art of selling is to look at its mechanics. So over the years, a lot of mechanical jargon grew up out of a sincere effort to understand the nature of the sale and breakdown the steps of a presentation into a mechanical sequence. It just seemed logical that if you knew the steps and took them all, you would make the sale. Right?

Looked at in this mechanical way, the presentation is simply a series of logical steps leading to a purchase.

There's the opening presentation (and a series of things you can do to perfect the perfect opening) and then there's the middle of the presentation (and another series of well-worn steps) and, of course, there's the closing of the presentation. There are scripts and steps and a lexicon of clever phrases to help you through all these mechanics.

Anyway that's what a lot of salespeople believe.

But have you ever wondered why, (if it's such a logical and progressive process), why is it that client's still say NO? If it's logical you should close 100% of the time. Do you close 100% of the time? If you do, you don't need help with your sales technique, you need a monument.

A mechanical approach can't be effective 100% of the time because all clients are different and have different ways of seeing things and have different requirements. So a mechanical presentation broken down into specific steps isn't going to be flexible enough to deal with all the various peculiarities that each individual buyer might have. Every buyer is different. No two people feel the exact same way about anything.

All buyers are human. And human beings are emotional creatures that can see a difference between one brand of soapsuds and another. As a result, we have dozens of different kinds of soaps, shampoos, laundry detergent, and cleaners. Can they all be so different? Often isn't it just the smell or the color that makes a difference? To some people it's the color that cinches the sale; to others, it's the smell. Everyone has his or her own reason.

A good salesperson knows how to take the client's feelings and works with them. The magic is taking your client's feelings and changing them in one direction or another by what you say. Once you understand how your client feels about your product from moment to moment, you can change your presentation to fit the client's feelings.

Think about this…if you know what your client is thinking as you make your presentation, and can see that the road you're going down isn't getting the job done, you can stop. There is no point going down this road if they aren't being impressed with it. Change direction. Try a different approach.

It's like they taught you in school. Stop, Look and Listen. By observing and carefully listening you can get where you want to go. Since you want to guide your client to a purchase, you need to know where you're going and that means you need a roadmap to help you.

Here's some good news ...that roadmap isn't locked away in a safe or surrounded by armed guards. What's amazing is that everything you need to know is not only easily available, it will be handed to you right during your meeting with your customer. You just have to know how to recognize it for what it is and then know what to do with it.

Sometime in the early 16tht century a Dutch sailing vessel was just off the coast of Brazil in serious condition. Their water had run out, their rations were depleted. The crew was dying. The charts in those times were so poor that the Captain had no idea where they were. Things looked pretty hopeless. Then a Spanish ship came over the horizon and the Dutchman raised his flags to beg for help.

"We have no water and are near death. Send help"

Within moments the reply came back:

"Lower your buckets and drink your fill."

The Spaniard knew what the Dutchman didn't. Both ships were at the mouth of the mighty Amazon River of Brazil. A river of such size and strength that it's fresh water carried miles beyond the coast into the sea. The seawater in which the Dutchman sailed was not salty at all. It was fresh. The captain just didn't know it. He didn't know what was actually all around him. And it nearly cost him dearly. Having the right information at the right time made the difference between life and death. And all it took was recognizing what was all around him.

I believe most of us are just like that Dutch sea captain. We are sailing in a river of information, but don't know how to lower that bucket to take advantage of it. That's fundamental to reading your client. It's a way to help you get that bucket down and retrieve the information that is all around you and use that information to make the sale. Often the hitch in the sale is a single thing and if you can figure it out... you make your sale.

Suppose you and I want to go fishing. The boat is tied to the dock with a rope. You take the oars and start rowing. The boat doesn't go very far because it's still tied to the dock. Now I can give you lots of reasons why we should go fishing. I can raise your desire to go fishing higher and higher. If I present really good reasons I can get you to row harder and harder but we still aren't going to go anywhere. Until we remove that rope that is restraining the boat we can't go anywhere.

That's what happens in lots of sales calls. The problem isn't with the presentation or with the desirability of the product. There's something restraining the sale. Remove the restraint and you make the sale.

How do you know what's restraining the sale? Sometimes it's pretty obvious . . . it's too expensive, it's not in the budget, it's not the right product, the buyer has no interest. Those obvious reasons can be addressed in a straightforward way.

If it's too expensive, we arrange payments. If it's not in the budget, we get the money from another budget. If it's not the right product, we show how the product is going to do just what the client wants. If the buyer has no interest, we try to get them interested.

But often a buyer is held back for a reason they would rather that you didn't know. These reasons are personal. They're emotional and that means they're very powerful. What kinds of reasons?

Every one of your clients is worried about his or her job. They want to advance; they want to be a success. Most importantly, they don't want to screw up. Your product gives them a chance to look good. But has it occurred to you that your product also gives them a chance to embarrass themselves in front of the entire company?

To you it's just a sale, another unit sold. But no matter how wonderful you think your product is...to the client it can potentially be a career stopper. What if it doesn't perform the way you expected it too? What if it doesn't perform the way THEY expected it too. Who's going to take the heat if the wheels come off?

Start Selling Smart! 23

Well, it won't be you because you'll be long gone. So who's left? It's going to be your customer and WOW if the wheels come off, they are going to remember it for a long time.

But let's assume that your product is going to perform just the way you said. After all it's been well built, and well tested and your company is going to stand behind it. There still are a lot of outside considerations that actually have nothing at all to do with you or your product that can influence your buyer and keep you from making a sale. We're all human and human beings have a million different things going through their heads at any given moment. Some are directly related to their business, but for every one of those there are lots of others that aren't.

Perhaps your customer has a real need for just the thing that you have. But what if today is the day he has a toothache or is worried about his kid's report card or is behind in his payments on his car? As unfair as it may seem, any of those things (and many more) can influence the way you and your product are going to be perceived. And none of it has anything to do with you.

All the things that happen in a typical business day can influence the way your customer is going to look at you and your product. What can you do about it? Some things you can deal with because they are directly related to business.

What if your customer has already gone over their budget? Perhaps they chronically go over budget. Here you come with your expensive widget (which they absolutely need and want,) tucked tightly under your arm. Even though it makes all kinds of logical sense for them to buy, they might defer.

It can leave you scratching your head wondering why. But the reason might be very simple. They might not want to buy the product because they are already over budget and are embarrassed to go to the boss and ask for more dough. What if the boss and your customer have already had words about cutting back and here you come with a budget breaker? You will get a cold shoulder for a reason that actually doesn't reflect on you or your product. It might simply just be the wrong item at the wrong time.

Is your product complicated or difficult to put into operation? If so you have a real problem. Because even though the buyer might love it, there are others who might not. Your customer might not be able to admit that the last time they bought something like this the sales department got upset because the salesmen couldn't figure out how to use it.

Your product and the sale are just as dependent on the current state of your customer's mind as it is on the value your product can provide. If either the value of your product or the attitude of your client isn't what they need it to be, you are not going to make a sale no matter how well you present.

So it's up to you to determine what is fixable and what is not. Business problems like budgets or time constraints can be handled. Things that are outside of your control such as his golf score or a toothache are not solvable. They aren't solvable because they are beyond your ability to change them. However all of those unsolvable problems have something in common. YOU don't have to allow them to influence your sale. You can isolate them. How?

CHAPTER TWO
SOLVING UNSOLVABLE PROBLEMS

Let's begin with the Unsolvable Problems first because the client will tell you right up front what they are. These don't require extrasensory perception to understand. If your client is bothered by something, he or she will have it on their mind. It will bother them and they will let you know about it. It will appear as something out of the ordinary. Like what?

If he or she says something like:

> *"It's been a bad day and I don't have a lot of time. Can you make this quick?"*

> or

> *"I just got called into a meeting in ten minutes can you give me a quick top line presentation?"*

You know that something has happen which has upset your customer's applecart and he or she is trying to clear the decks to deal with it. So they will ask you to change your presentation to match their situation. It certainly is a reasonable request. But, this is something that you cannot control. Things happen all the time. The problem in this case is you need that time to do your job. They don't have the time. What should you do? Your first impression is to be a nice guy and agree to a quick presentation but, STOP and think for a moment. If you do that, you will have a distracted customer, a partial presentation and no real opportunity to discuss the product. If you are agreeable and do what they want, they will be happy, but you will undoubtedly lose this sale

SMART SELLING

IF THEY DON'T HAVE TIME FOR YOU

GET OUT AND GET OUT FAST.

No one has to go forward with a presentation if the timing just isn't going to work. You get one shot at making a sale and if it's the wrong time, then accept it as just that. Remember it is your duty to control this meeting. It's your meeting.

You are trying to do a job here and if you can't do it, then get out and try another day. If the buyer has a bad cold that you feel will make it difficult for you to make your sale, then postpone the meeting. Don't just go through the motions because you want to get this prospect off your list.

In other words the moment you get out of the car or pick up the phone you have to be in charge. You must start selling from the very first moment. If the client throws up a roadblock that will make it impossible for you to do your job...don't go forward.

"But..."

you're thinking,

"It took me two months to nail this guy down. You want me to walk away?"

Yes that's about the size of it. He or she has dropped the ball, not you. So chances are they will reschedule when it's more convenient, but not in two months. Take the opportunity to put it directly to them:

"Ohh, that's too bad. We'll such things happen. How about meeting tomorrow (or next week or soon).That way you can take care of this crisis properly. I won't mind.

Looked at from another direction...if you let them change your presentation, they are in control, not you. You can't let anything they do interfere with making your presentation, just the way you want. So don't let them. Be nice. Be firm. Be in control from the first moment until you walk out the door.

Being nice isn't going to earn you one single brownie point and it will cost you a sale. You have a job to do and it's your duty to do it, as well as you can.

I don't know how many times I have heard salespeople complain that the reason they didn't make the sale was because the client didn't appreciate the product's benefits.

Hello? That was their job! They are hired to present the product's benefits. If they didn't do that then they screwed up their own sale. It wasn't the client's fault! If the client doesn't understand something it is the salesperson, who has failed. And the most likely reason is that the salesperson either didn't have enough time to cover the benefits or the client was not receiving what the salesperson was saying *because they were thinking of something else!*

Well, you can pitch all day and all night and if no one is catching, there really isn't a ball game going on is there?

How do you protect yourself from this?

If you don't have the client's full attention before you begin, then the first thing you must do is try to find out how to get their attention. Know why before presenting. If they are telling you they don't really want to listen, then believe them. Don't just go into automatic presentation mode. It's over and you might as well pack up your tent and quietly steal away.

Yes, I know sometimes it takes months to set up a pitch. But if the client isn't completely in the same room with you...you aren't making a pitch!. You're just going through the motions.

I had a boss who said it very well. He played high school football and when the team faced a much stronger team, one that they knew they couldn't beat, they would "Look good... losing" They would put up a half hearted sort of fight, so they wouldn't look too bad, even though they knew they weren't going to win.

Be careful trying to look good losing. It's an easy habit to fall into. Sure, you're tired, it's been a long day. You have just this one last call and you can pack it in. Just one more push and now this mini emergency happens which can screw the entire presentation up.

You would be much smarter to just go home. If you don't know you are going to have the client's full attention, waiting to listen, don't pitch.

A salesman never looks good losing. It's impossible. Either you make the sale or you don't. There are no excuses for not making the sale. It is your job to make the sale, not find reasons why the sale couldn't be made.

Sometimes things happen right in the middle of a presentation .If they say:

"Oh Gosh! We just got a last minute rush order. I've got to get it out pronto. Can you make this quick?"

Say *"No"* and leave. Obviously, do it with some grace and finesse. But the bottom line is that you only present when the client wants to hear what you have to say and has the time to actually pay attention.

There is no point in going to a meeting where the client is forced into listening out of courtesy. I assure you, they won't buy out of courtesy. By giving an abbreviated pitch, you are just trying to look good losing and that's not where you want to be. Give yourself a fair chance to make the sale.

Selling is a profession that requires a lot of discipline to be done well. That discipline is mainly in keeping your emotions under control and your client satisfied. It takes a bit of juggling. But that doesn't mean that your customer is doing you a great service by allowing you into their august presence. The truth is you have something they need. You wouldn't be there if they didn't need something like what you have to sell.

Remember

SMART SELLING

IF THEY AGREED TO MEET

THEY NEED WHAT YOU HAVE TO SELL

You are helping them out, not the other way around. You are a professional and your time is valuable as well. They have their business to run and you have yours. If they have invited you to make a presentation, then they have the obligation to sit there and listen to what you have to tell them. If something unavoidable happens which makes it difficult to properly present, you have every right in the world to reschedule so you can do your job properly.

Doing that job requires much more than a little black book of potential buyers and the dogged determination to work from the first page all the way to the last page as efficiently as possible. It is actually much more important than page turning.

Each meeting is a chance to not only make a sale, but to develop a mutually beneficial relationship. You are an asset your customer can benefit from. If your product works the way you say it will, they benefit. It will make them look good. So if they don't give you enough time to do the job right, then it's up to you to back away and allow yourself the opportunity to do it right.

You wouldn't tell the pilot to land the plane in a hurry because you were in a rush, would you? You wouldn't ask the radiologist to just glance over your MRI because you had a meeting. You recognize they have a job to do and the expertise to do it well. That's why you picked them. The same applies to you. Or at least you should go into your meeting with your client convinced that you are a professional with the credentials to back up everything you say.

If your client feels they have to bump you for an uncontrollable reason that's unavoidable then there is nothing personal intended and you shouldn't take it personally. But if they feel you're just a nuisance that has to be listened to, then you've made a fundamental error in setting the meeting up in the first place.

They should be looking forward to meeting with you and to hearing about your product. You can accomplish that with Smart Selling. Smart Selling allows you to position yourself in such a way that the client will do whatever they can to make sure they have the time to listen to what you have to say and the ability to make a decision about it.

In a bit we will use Smart Selling in setting up the meeting in the first place. If you do it right you can walk into the meeting with confidence, knowing that they are going to be eager to hear what you have to say and ready to pay close attention.

CHAPTER THREE
WONDERFUL LAST WORDS

Once you have your customer ready to listen, you need to be tuned to signals that hint at difficulty that your sale might face. As we discussed above when we used the example of the boat tied to the dock, sometimes, silent reasons can restrain your sale. You have the responsibility to determine what the rope that is tying you to the dock is. But here's the good part. Your client will help you..

If you really have a product that the buyer recognizes as being of value, then they will try to find a way to make your product fit. If they have some silent reason for not telling you straight out why they are hesitating, they often will try to send you a message in a round about way so they can enlist your help. To be able to read what your client is saying, you need Smart Selling. Here's what I mean:

Our buyer has a dilemma. On the one hand, they want what it is you have, on the other, they are restrained by one reason or another. To make matters worse they won't tell you any of this. They might have a myriad of reasons to hesitate, perhaps it might embarrass them or might reveal too much about their vulnerability Since the reason is hidden, it's probably an emotional one, which means of course, that it's not logical or rational and since business is supposed to run in a dispassionate and logical way, your client will come up with a substitute reason. One that will only seem to be dispassionate and reasonable. But remember, it won't be the real reason but it will seem like a reason.

These substitute reasons can be pretty frustrating. I'm sure you've heard these from time to time, but perhaps you never gave them a thought. The most frequent one is

"I like it, let me ask my boss and get back to you."

Then there is always:

"Wow this is really great. Give me some time to think about it.

Now doesn't this sound promising?

How often do you hear:

"Wow…this is really great! But…"

Don't kid yourself. Statements like this are big trouble. I call them 'wonderful last words'.

You are not going to get this sale if you stop at this point. These are not complements. These are excuses for not buying. Getting past excuses like this is your job. These "reasons" are actually not reasons at all. They are a way to keep the door open and close it at the same time. They don't want to commit. This is a signal that you have to read right. It sounds real nice but it's purely poison. They will never get back to you. When you call, they will turn you down. They didn't commit.

There is one unshakeable truth in sales:

SMART SELLING

NO COMMITMENT ...NO SALE.

It's that simple. OK if you haven't gotten the commitment what do you do?

There's a reason they are not committing. Something is restraining the sale. If you knew what it was, you could free them from the restraint and the sales would proceed normally. Contrary to what you might think your customer isn't trying to keep the real reason from you. They might not even be consciously aware of what the reason is. If you asked them, they would probably say they just wanted to have time to turn it over in their mind.

Let's stop and think about their excuses for a minute.

"Give me some time to think about it"

What exactly is there to think out? If you laid out all the sales points and they have a real need for what your product does, the logic of the situation should be obvious. But that's just it, isn't it? It's NOT logical it's emotional.

Aren't they telling you two contradictory things? Asking for more time says *"yes"* and *"no"* at the same time. They might commit, then again, they might not.

What kind of an answer is that? Something hasn't been verbalized. It's silent. It's in code. And you have to "decode" what is bothering them. Fortunately, you can! You can, if you pay attention and use Smart Selling.

To find the hot button sales point, you look for signals that they will give to you as you speak and as you listen and observe. If you ever read the stories by Sir Arthur Conan Doyle about his famous detective character, Sherlock Holmes, you will notice that Holmes solves crimes by observing the little things such as the splashes of mud on a sleeve or the trace of cigar ash in the corner. These little things speak very clearly and when taken together build a picture of what actually happened. These insignificant things are very difficult to hide. Because the character that created them was unaware of them. For all intents and purposes they were unconscious.

So you must become a detective, You start listening and seeing things carefully. You are looking for that broken twig or for something out of place. Start as soon as you walk in the door, throughout your meeting and as you leave. You remain on watch the entire time and pay attention to what is going on all around you. That's where all the information is. That's what you have to put into that bucket we talked about earlier.

This is quite different than a traditional sales call where the sales person sits there and waits for his meeting and gives his pitch and goes on to the next call. Such 'salespeople" aren't actually in sales. They are just going down a list of prospects. He or she is actually worse off, since even with their eyes open he or she is fast asleep. They are paying attention to nothing. The only thing they might be paying any attention to at all is their presentation and the only thing they are wondering about is how that presentation is going to help close this deal. As we mentioned earlier:

Traditional salespeople never really focus on the client; they focus on their product. It's a mistake. They need to sell the customer not the product.

So what is it that you should be looking for to determine when you are being handed one of those wonderful last words which means:

"Good bye I'm not committing to a thing".

The most typical type of restraint that is going to motivating your customer is:

"How will it make me look?"

They have a reputation to protect. They have their job to protect. If they're responsible for purchasing widgets like the ones you sell, then they better know a bit about getting the best widget for the job. Right?

Perhaps what is restraining your customer is their fear that your widget might make them look bad.

Every purchase or decision they make, puts them in the spotlight. So every decision is potentially a risk. Even if they approve of your product, there are others who they have to report to. Each of those people are going to ask the same question.

"Why"
"Why did you purchase this?
"Why did you decide to go with this company?"

Why? Why? Why?" And your client has to defend that choice. So you have an obligation to leave him or her with something they can use to answer that inevitable question . . . why? Your job is to protect your sale by giving your customer some ammunition to fight with. Once you leave there will be no one to fight for your sale.

We all have someone we must answer to.

If someone who works for a company made the purchase, then the person they have to answer to is . . . the boss. If your client buys something the company needs and he or she can show the boss that they figured out that need and filled it, then the boss is going to be satisfied, they are doing their job well. If they can't, they have a big problem because their boss is going to start wondering about how capable they are.

So what do you do? If you think the reason they are not committing is because your product might make them look bad, you must convince them that it will not. That means reassuring them that the product has worked successfully in lots of other cases. Quote sales figures and sales increases from those companies that used it. Present endorsements. Stress your money back, triple bottomed, no fail, no question guarantee. Offer to personally come and fix it, if it breaks. Do whatever you have to do to assure them that the product will make them look good.

This logic also applies to asking for a raise or buying a new car or making any serious decision. In the case of a single person making a serious decision or a serious purchase, they have somebody they have to answer to. In that case, that "person" is their conscience. We all have a self-image to uphold. We all want to think we have good judgment and are reasonable in our expectations and desires. If we do something that bothers our conscience then, we regret it.

That regret is called "buyers remorse." Buyer's remorse is what you go through when you wake up in the middle of the night and say:

> "Oh man, why did I buy that (car, pool table, coat, etc)? I should never have done it. I'm going to take it back"

How many times has that happened to you?

If you're like most people, it has happened lots of times. Everyone feels the same way. You want something but you're afraid it will make you look bad. So you waffle back and forth. *'Yes, I do, but I really shouldn't. But I really would like to. But I'll feel bad. Etc. '*

Do you know what you most likely will do? Nothing. You won't commit. Easy isn't it? You as the buyer are off the hook. But of course, this is not good for you, if you are the salesman

Your client isn't going to buy anything that he or she can't defend to either:

1. themselves or

2. to the boss as being the absolutely right item. So as a salesperson you actually have two jobs.

The first is to make the buyer feel good about you, your product and your company. You do this by providing answers to anything that stands between you and your sale. And the second job is to provide your customer with a good reason to justify their decision.

What is that?

SMART SELLING

GIVE THEM A REALLY GOOD REASON TO BUY.

Something, which they can take to the boss and hold up and say:

> " *I did this for the right reason.*
>
> *I feel good about buying this.*
>
> *AND HERE'S THE REASON WHY"*

This works every time. Use yourself as an example. If you have a really good reason to buy that magnificent new red sports car, then you are going to go ahead and buy. The reason doesn't have to be earth shattering.

It might be that you think you deserve a reward for working so hard, or maybe the deal is too good to turn down or perhaps it's something that you feel will make you more successful, so that it's really an "investment" instead of an "expense". Whatever the reason is...you have to believe it. It has to be a solid, believable reason. And if you have it...you commit.

In most cases, the reason they are going to deliver that *wonderful last word* to you, is simply they need a really, good reason to buy. And for some reason, you haven't found it yet. The solution is then ...FIND IT.

CHAPTER FOUR
WHEN THEY ALWAYS TELL YOU THE TRUTH

It's amazing how much clients will reveal about what is going on in their minds, which they don't realize they are revealing. As we speak we think and in general edit out the things we are thinking which we don't want the other person to know. However in the give and take of most conversations often it is difficult to completely disguise what you really think because your choice of words gives you away. So it's very important to listen closely to the exact words and phrasing that your customer is speaking. This is SMART SELLING.

Selling isn't a game. It's serious business. The conversation might seem to be very calm and relaxed, but there is a lot going on behind your customer's eyeballs that bear directly on you making your sale. Most salespeople just hear words and think that's all there is. If you ask them what went on during the sales call they will say something like:

> "Oh it went pretty well. I gave them the pitch and they seemed to like it. They told me they would try to give me a call on Wednesday."

You know what? The phone will not ring next Wednesday and the average salesperson will wonder why. And the reason the phone will not ring is because the salesperson didn't really know what was going on at the meeting in the first place. They only heard about half the meeting because they just judged the meeting by what the client said, not by what the client didn't say.

Obviously the most important thing the client can say is:

"I'll buy it."

That's a commitment. That's what you are supposed to walk out of the meeting with. So if you don't get a commitment but an excuse for delaying the commitment, then you haven't had a good meeting. This is not to say that you won't make the sale. You still might get the sale, but promises aren't the same thing as purchases.

Has this ever happened to you? You are making a presentation and everyone is having a great time and laughing and smiling and they never buy the product? Or how about the opposite, where you make a lousy presentation, your jokes fall flat and no one seems to react at all and magically somehow they say:

"OK we'll buy. Where's the paperwork?"

Either outcome can happen but it's not dependent on what is said in the meeting but what is thought in the meeting. You've got to understand what they are thinking. To do so you have to listen to what the say <u>and</u> to what they don't say. Both are equally important.

Certainly some of their thoughts are revealed by what they are saying to you, But you must listen as well for certain statements or questions that should be covered. If they are not said, there could be trouble.

So what are those things?

Every successful meeting must cover some pretty basic items and they ordinarily come in a specific order

1. They need to know about what the product does and how it is better than the competitions or their present product.

2. They need to know about your company and how reliable your company is.

3. They need to feel you are ready and able to give them the kind of service they are going to need.

4. Depending upon what the product is they should want it to be able to slip into their operation without a lot of down time and extra training.

5. They need to know that the product will hold up and not cause problems.

6. Lastly the value has to be in the product and worth what you are asking for it. In short they need to believe that the value is worth the price.

Now there is no reason to ask how much something is going to cost (#6) if the product can't pass steps #1-5. So if they haven't asked all of those questions in one form or another and the meeting concludes...you haven't finished your sales presentation and there is no reason for them to buy.

This means you must cover all these key points and convince them that every single step is covered. That's the minimum. There can be all kinds of extra inducements, special pricing, promotions, features etc. but they are not central to the sale. Those blandishments just make the sale easier. It's the core that must be solid before you can make the sale.

First and foremost the sale doesn't depend upon everyone's demeanor. Happy people in a meeting don't necessarily make sales happen. Sure, you want to have a good relationship with your client. That's just common sense. But being pleasant is not going to get your product sold. If your product does its job well and your client is satisfied than that is what will keep your client happy. They expect results not a warm smile and a pleasant manner.

So just because they tell you how wonderful you are and how much they enjoyed your presentation doesn't mean they are going to buy. It means that they didn't mind spending some time with you. However you aren't selling your time and glowing personality, you are selling your product.

In the example above the meeting ended pleasantly. The customer liked the product and said so. They like the presentation and said so. But those comments don't close the sale. To find out if they are going to buy or not, you have to listen to what they say and what they don't say. You have to hear what they want you to hear and you have to determine what they are thinking as well. This takes much more than just listening. It takes sensitivity to what they are doing and saying, as they talk.

Shortly, you will see how what seems to be ordinary conversation can take on an entirely different meaning than what you might imagine. But first we need to understand a little bit about the way we communicate. It's not as simple as opening your mouth and letting words fall out. In human affairs, words are very carefully chosen because in any meeting, it is important not to offend the other by overstating your feelings. So even though you might feel negatively toward a person, you will be careful to hide that feeling.

Has a client ever said to you:

"Are you crazy!
That's the nuttiest idea I ever heard.
Get out of my office!"

Now I'd call that a pretty obvious verbal expression wouldn't you? But of course, clients aren't going to say that to you even if they feel that way. A harsh verbal statement like that is going to make you mad. It's going to lead to a lot of shouting and banging on the table and a very upsetting experience. They don't want that even if they think you are a complete lunatic. So they will avoid a confrontation and just try to hustle you out of the office. They will look at their watch, snap their fingers and say:

" Oh gee, look at the time I just remembered...I have a meeting with the Chairman of the Board and the entire Board of Directors in 10 minutes."

Really now. Do you think they REALLY have a meeting with the COB and the entire Board of Directors?

The excuse they make up is a way to avoid a conflict. They don't want to tell you the truth. They just want to get you out of there. So . . . they make up an excuse.

Have you ever thanked your hostess after a dreary party and said:

"Thank you for inviting me, I had a wonderful time"

when in fact you couldn't wait to get out of there?

What do you do when the waiter asks:

"Is everything alright?"

when your soup is cold and the steak is tough? Often we just nod and say:

"Everything's' fine."

It's not fine. We just wasted a wad of cash on a mediocre meal, but it just isn't worth getting involved with a lot of explanations. If we complain about the soup or the steak we know they will take it back and try to fix it, but we're hungry and that will mean going all the way back to the beginning. So we smile (even though we don't actually feel good) and we say:

"Everything's fine"

and then we frown as we look down at our plate. If someone were sitting across the table, they would know that you were unhappy.

If you could see yourself you would know that a lot of what you were saying was baloney. So don't you imagine it might be possible that people will react the same way in a presentation? Of course they do. So use it. That's SMART SELLING. Read their reaction to what you say and don't assume what they say is the entire message. Watch what they are doing as much as well as listen to what they are saying.

In a similar vein, there is one special time when they will always tell you the truth. When that occurs it can be worth a lot of shoe leather that would otherwise be wasted if you don't realize it.

That one very important moment comes at the end of the meeting. This moment is extremely important because they are going to tell you how well you did.

You've made your pitch, they asked all their questions, you gave them answers. Now they are going to say something and it will probably be the truth. It can happen at anytime-As you are walk to the door-As you get into your car.

It's just before you leave. Now why would they tell you the truth at the end of the meeting?

Let's look at the facts from their point of view. The client has invited you over to show them your product. If you made them look good by doing a good job, they are going to want to let you know they appreciate that. So they'll say:

"Thanks for coming. It was a fine presentation and I think Joe (the SR VP of whatever) really was impressed."

What your host is actually saying is that he knows Joe and he knows Joe's quirks and body language and your host is letting you in on his read of the outcome. He's saying Joe liked it. Which probably means you've got a shot at a sale.

If, on the other hand, your host says:

"Thanks for coming. I think Joe liked everything but...

(the return on investment data. Etc)"

Then you know you have a problem with an unanswered question that you must have left lying about on the conference room floor. That's serious!

You can't leave any unanswered questions lying about. If you missed an important point in your presentation or didn't answer a question that they needed answered, they will begin to speculate. And that means TROUBLE! Why?

You'll be gone, happily whistling to yourself as you drive back to the office, thinking that everything is just peachy and they will be wondering why you didn't tell them where your main distribution centers are. And that's a big problem for them. They will then begin to think that you omitted this information on purpose because you're main distribution point is in Zaire!

That does it. No one in his or her right mind is going to take this idea forward until this entire distribution system set up is solved.

So any unanswered question is really big trouble. Any unanswered question will grow into a really serious problem. If the SR VP is worried or puzzled or uncomfortable, you have a very big problem no matter how small the problem might seem to you. So that little line ...*everything but*... is most assuredly going to kill your deal unless you can get it cleared up immediately.

That's why it's so important to know when they are telling you the truth. If they don't reveal their concerns to you while you are there...you can't answer them and then all hell breaks lose because unanswered questions start to grow and they become major conflagrations in seconds.

I've found these little "bye bye" sentences so revealing that I put them in a special category. Unlike whatever they might say during a meeting, whatever smiles they give you, whatever promises they make; I've found that as you walk out of the building they always tell you something that is not only true but generally important.

I've summed up this observation with this phrase and I'd like you to pay special attention to it because you will find it very useful. Here it is . . .

SMART SELLING

THEY ALWAYS TELL YOU THE TRUTH AT THE END

They tell you the truth because it's over and you either are coming back or you are not coming back. The presentation either went well or it didn't. And since you're leaving they don't have to be careful about holding anything back. If they liked it and liked you and think you might be back, they'll tell you so. They have no reason to remain coy about it. You've convinced them. So they'll tell you and start to build a relationship.

"Say that was a terrific presentation you made and I think Joe thought your widget has a lot of possibilities."

Obviously, this is good. But what if they say:

*"Say thanks for coming over.
We'll think about it and get back to you."*

Notice . . . nothing about you, nothing about the product, and nothing about their reaction, nothing about what they are feeling. This statement tells you absolutely nothing except *"thanks"*. No commitment to any future contact. Which, unfortunately, probably means there is not going to be any future contact. You are being dismissed.

But what if they say something like this?

"Say that was a terrific presentation. Joe and I will be getting together on Wednesday to look into that pay-out schedule you gave us. We both are worried about this but... maybe we can work it out, then we'll be getting back to you."

They liked the presentation. Joe and your host are willing to talk, but obviously there is a problem. Now the door isn't closed completely, but you did leave a problem behind. Sometimes you can't solve it. But at least you are aware of it, so perhaps you can send over some data or offer to discuss it at lunch before the client gets together with his boss. Whatever the problem if it's on their mind, you will hear about it sooner or later.

No one likes to turn someone down cold, flat. It's painful. So they could be preparing you for the bad news by hinting at it now. It's the truth. So you are left in mid air wondering if you made a sale or not. The important thing to remember is that they want you to succeed. It's just this pay-out schedule (or whatever it is) that is restraining them. They would like you to help in some way. If you can, your host thinks you can make this sale.

Notice in all three cases the client may have been very pleasant, everyone might have smiled and laughed and enjoyed the conversation. That has little to do with putting the pen to paper and closing the deal.

There are a number of other hints you can pick up as the meeting comes to a close, which will give you some valuable insights into what they did and didn't like about you, your company and your product. Listen for statements like this.

"Gee your company has a great reputation"

(This means that they like the idea of their company matched to your company. A very good sign.)

"You know production is going to appreciate how easy it will be to put this on the line"

(This means that they think they can convince production not to put up too much of a fuss)

"Send me some information on that reliability testing you did."

(You struck a nerve with that line. They want to know more about it)

That's their way of saying that they are impressed enough to give it serious consideration. They aren't being polite. They are being serious. That's what you want to hear.

But if they don't say anything about any of these points but confine themselves to pleasantries such as.

> "Thanks for making the long drive. Have a nice trip home."

Oh boy you made the trip for nothing. Don't sit up nights wondering how you did. You're dead.

Is it really worthwhile to spend all this effort reading into what your client says and does at a meeting? Won't they sooner or later tell you either 'yes' or 'no'? Probably they will tell you something sooner or later. The answer relates to your efficiency.

The reason it is worth the effort is because too often salespeople spend years in a fog wondering why this account didn't click or that sale fell through. They don't understand why they are failing to make important sales. They spin their wheels traveling down a road trying to make a dead deal come alive. As a salesperson you have only a limited amount of time. You need to cut through the baloney that fogs the presentation and come up with a realistic appraisal of where you stand. If you aren't going to make the sale, then at least you will know it and you can get on with your next call.

Realistically not every sale is possible. Some clients are just not going to buy no matter how clever and attentive you are. They are time wasters. And they can cost you and your company a lot of money. You can find out by making useless sales calls and waste time waiting by the phone or you can use your time efficiently.

SMART SELLING is much more efficient because it focuses you on making sales that are real, rather than ones that are impossible. Earlier we mentioned that sometimes things get in the way, which just make it impossible to present.

Sometimes clients are just impossible to sell too. This moment, when they always tell you the truth will help you determine if you have one of those clients. Obviously if you don't have a prayer of making this sale, you don't want to be sitting by the telephone tapping your fingers wondering why they don't call. Instead you should be on to your next presentation where you'll be applying SMART SELLING to get the next sale.

CHAPTER FIVE
THE SINGLE MOST IMPORTANT QUESTION

Let's say that you represent the GIZMO widget company and you have been making a presentation. You've reeled off all your sales points about the WIDGET 101 and have impressed them with your credentials. Let's say that then the most senior person in the room asks:

"How much is it?"

You tell them the price and they say:

"Isn't that an awful lot?"

Now isn't this as normal as scrambled eggs? Isn't this what most people would say? What could you get out of this very straightforward question? Believe it or not you are within inches of making a sale. That is IF you understand what the client is really saying. Most salespeople would blow their sale sky high at this point. but using SMART SELLING you can close this sale.

Here's why:

What is the single most important question a client must ask?

The most important question a client can ask is ...

"How much?"

They have to ask about price.

If the client hasn't asked about price, they are not yet convinced that they want to make a purchase. Why waste your breath asking about how much it costs, if you're not going to buy it?

In this case, they are asking you about price very near the beginning of the pitch. That's odd because in most cases you have to build up a case to get them to ask about price. So since the most senior man has already asked the most important question, you know they are VERY interested in making a purchase. They would never do that if they were uncomfortable with you, your company or your product. So they must already be comfortable with all those things, The customer is already at HOW MUCH. That's a long way down in the list of standard and inevitable questions. It's generally right at the end.

So that's how you know that you're close to a close. You did what you were supposed to do (or someone else has already done it for you).

Either way your credibility is established and they are impressed enough with you and your product that they are not asking those standard and inevitable questions which must be asked.

So they move on to the really big question. HOW MUCH? This is indeed a good sign.. However it's the second statement that they make:

"Isn't that an awful lot?"

which has the potential to blow this absolutely beautiful sale sky high. This is without a doubt the most critical part of this entire conversation. You might not be aware of it, but more sales are lost at this point than at any other point of a presentation. And that's because salespeople don't understand what a client is actually asking.

To most sales people when a client asks a question in this way:

Isn't that an awful lot?
Don't you think this will be hard to use?
Isn't that going to take a long time?
Why would you need that?

They think the client wants an answer. So they give the standard answer.

Isn't that an awful lot?

Is answered by

We feel we're priced competitively

———————————

Don't you think this will be hard to use?

Is answered by

No it's actually very easy to use.

———————————

Isn't that going to take a long time?

Is answered by

It's quite a customary length of time

———————————

Why would you need that?

Is answered by

It's our standard operating procedure.

If you think about all these client questions for a moment you will see that the client isn't asking for an answer, they are asking you for more information or perhaps your opinion. They want you to tell them what you think. Why are they asking you what you think? Because (now pay attention here since this is the essence of a SMART SELLING approach)

They want a good reason to buy your product.

They want you to give them an iron clad, copper bottomed, triple distilled reason to buy that we discussed in Chapter 3. Why?

To stop the boss dead in his tracks when the boss asks them that very same question.

Boss:

> *Jones, Isn't that going to be hard to use?*

Jones:

> *Boss I'm glad you asked me that because this widget is one of the easiest widgets the Gizmo Company has ever designed. The salesman told me that they conducted three years of research to make sure that any child under the age of 10 could understand how to use it within 5 minutes. I'll tell you, Boss, it was impressive.*

This is the moment you should be praying for. When they spring that "don't you think" sort of question on you, they are looking for a few words as a closer. They are begging you for ammo.

And for goodness sake give it to them!

Here's why SMART SELLING works. With that question they have told you much more than the average salesperson would realize. Now you know that they are setting themselves up to become your ally, your defender, your buddy.

Most salespeople wouldn't get it. Most sales people won't recognize that the question is rhetorical and believe it or not will answer the question as if it were seriously meant. So they will go down their handy dandy list of sales points and routine responses and to the question

> *Don't you think that's an awful lot??*

 They will say:

> *We feel we're priced competitively*

Well isn't that terrific? The salesperson has given an answer to a question that really didn't exist. It was a rhetorical question. It would have been much better to just say nothing at all than to start becoming confrontational. Now our goofy salesperson is letting this very interested customer slip out of their fingers.

Start Selling Smart!

Here's how.

The standard answer that they gave was:

We feel we're priced competitively"

That answer doesn't give the client anything to defend the product with. It's not what they are going to need when he or she is standing in front of the boss, So that's bad.

But what's worse is that it's argumentative. Our sales person is saying to the customer:

" NO! You're wrong it's worth every penny."

So now the salesperson is disagreeing with the client. Why in the world would any sales person, worth their salt, go out of their way to disagree with the client? Don't they realize that starting an argument with the client isn't going to make this sale for them? You don't want them to get mad. You don't want a shouting match. Selling is agreement not argument.

Our average Joe salesman is now roaring along, paddling just as fast as he can go and doesn't realize he is headed over the falls by following this well worn script.

Client:

> *It's too much.*

Salesman:

> *No It's Not!*

Client:

> *YES IT IS.*

Salesman:

> *NO IT'S NOT!*

Is this a way to make a sale? What salesman school did this guy come from?

This whole thing becomes even more alarming when we realize that this confrontation is exactly the opposite of what the customer wanted. After all if the customer wanted disagreement they wouldn't have asked for an opinion, they would have just simply said:

> *"That's too much"* or

> *"Sorry I don't have the budget for that"*

or something which would very convincingly end the conversation. They wouldn't ask for an opinion. There would be no room for doubt.

"Sorry that's too much. I'll take my business elsewhere."

But they didn't do that. They don't want to take their business elsewhere. They want a reason to justify the price. Our salesperson is close to convincing them but the client has a boss to report to. What are they going to say when their boss glares at them and demands to know why they blew so much on this widget? It's your job to give them the ammunition not an argument. They are actually saying something like:

"I like you and I trust your opinion. It seems to me that that's a heck of a lot of money for this item. Now, I like it and I would buy it if I had a good enough reason to pay that much for it. But I'm not sure that it's worth the price. "Isn't that an awful lot?" What do you think? "

Who knows, maybe there is a good reason for charging so much. Maybe it has a 24 karat jeweled movement. Maybe it's made of platinum. Maybe this WIDGET will do things never believed possible. Maybe.

But the way our standard sales person is going to react to this is to just read the surface, the actual words.

Misreading this is bad, but unfortunately it gets worse. This superficial interpretation is going to bring the sales person to a conclusion that will color ALL the future business they might do with this customer and their company. This error therefore has some big time consequences. What conclusion is that? By misreading what the client was asking, they are going to jump to the conclusion that the client is "dumb."

In a huff they will repeat to themselves something like this:

"Isn't this an awful lot?

What a stupid question. Why would they ask me if I thought it was too expensive?
OF COURSE the item is not too expensive. It's worth exactly what it's worth. Hmmmmph.

Don't these people realize how difficult it is to make a 24 karat gold platted Widget like this. How dumb can you be? Do they think these widgets just grow on a tree?"

Now our foggy headed sales person is paddling down the river in the wrong direction. They think the client doesn't like the product (which we know is just the opposite of what the client is saying) AND that the client has a screw loose to ask such a provocative question (which we know is just the opposite of what the situation actually is). This misinterpretation is not the client's fault. It's the sales persons fault and they are going right over the falls for no reason.

Now this is pathetic. And it happens all the time. The client sincerely wants to hear more, not slam the door. The salesman completely misses the point and now thinks the client is stupidly provocative. The sales person gives the standard answer, one that is practically guaranteed to light the fuse that will begin a confrontation and ultimately a shouting match.

What a mess!

This could have been a golden opportunity to present all the reasons the product is worth every penny. That would have gotten the client agreeing. The customer would be soaking it all up. Loading up for that ultimate confrontation with his boss. This could have been a closing opportunity and instead it is blowing this deal wide open. The salesperson was actually inches from a close. But by the time they realize it this sale will have gone a glimmering. Just a few words of explanation might have gotten a much more positive response from the client. Here' what I mean.

Customer:

> *Isn't that an awful lot?*

You:

That's a good question. Yes, it is a lot more than our competition. But there's a very good reason. Our Widgets are actually gold plated in all their internal workings.

Most of our competitors use brass. And brass will work but it's really a question of longevity. Brass won't hold up the way our gold plated bearings will. And because they are gold plated they roll much better actually increasing the time between routine maintenance.

Now if you don't care about down time for routine maintenance then perhaps you'd be satisfied with simple brass. Our model 5 is all brass. It's somewhat cheaper. But it also has about 1/3rd the working life.

Gizmo has been in the Widget biz for over 100 years and we've sold a lot of Widgets as you might imagine. So we can accommodate you no matter what your requirements. We can do either brass or gold. Which would you rather have?

Customer:

> *"Oh I see...gold plated! My oh my. . .*

> *well I didn't know that."*

All it would have taken is a little sensitivity on the part of the sales person to see beyond the words into what the client was really asking. Not only would it avoid a confrontation it might just have saved this sale.

CHAPTER SIX
THINGS ARE SELDOM WHAT THEY SEEM?

Earlier we went over how important it was to give your client ammunition so they could defend their purchase in front of the boss. Generally customers couch these information-seeking questions in a particular way and it usually appears in a pattern that you can learn to identify. It can be a big help when determining how best to answer what may seem like an innocent question but which has the power to spin out of control.

Watch out for questions, which are presented in the following form. First there's a question which often starts with: HOW MUCH and after you respond is immediately followed up with: IS THAT or ISN'T THAT or DON'T YOU THINK...

So it looks like this:

Client:

> *How long does it take to install?*

Salesman:

> *Two weeks*

Client:

> *DON'T YOU THINK that's an awfully long time?*

Client:

> *How Much training will be required?*

Salesman:

We provide you with 30 days of free technical support

Client:

> *IS THAT the same as your competition?*

Client:

> *How long is your warranty?*

Salesman:

> *30 days parts and labor is standard*

Client:

> *ISN'T THAT awfully short?*

This repeating pattern generally exposes an underlying issue, you would be wise to address. They like you, they like the product but they have this worry and what are you going to do about it?

It's a little dance that you both do. It's a verbal gesture, which is meant to give you a clue that more information is needed. Once you learn to recognize the form it's as clear as an SOS. They want an opinion not a statement.

The only problem with the dance is that most sales people don't know they are dancing. They are so wrapped up in their presentation and how good they want to look; they don't listen to what the client is really saying. Here's where SMART SELLING can really be useful.

Watch out for questions, which come in a particular place in your presentation where they are not expected or shouldn't be. They can be very revealing as well. As an example:

Here you are sailing along, presenting your WIDGET to the ACME Company and right in the middle of your presentation, just at the good part (when you start talking about how efficient it is in comparison with the FOGHORN WIDGET) they interrupt you and ask:

"How long have you been selling widgets?"

What does it mean?

Let's look at the facts. This is a question that is actually off the mark of an inquiry about the product. This isn't about the widget's price or it's construction or it's warranty. This question is about you. Why are they asking about you? Before you read on . . . think about it from the client's point of view.

Since this is a question about your experience, the buyer isn't yet comfortable with your credibility. They want to know how much experience you have. Why would they do that? They aren't going to ask for advice from someone who hasn't much experience. So *"How long have you been selling widgets?"* means they want to know how much of what we say is based on experience and how much came from our list of handy sales points.

This has big implications. They are inquiring about your fitness to come aboard as a consultant. Suddenly in an odd sort of way they are asking for your resume. You are being considered for a promotion from salesman to consultant. That's why the need for "deep" background.

That's why it comes right in the middle of your presentation. They like what they are hearing and are wondering out loud if it's because you're really good or your sales points are really good. How do they find out? Clearly they can't ask: *"Say are you really good or do you just read your list well?"* can they?

So they get at the information in an indirect way. They start by getting more information about you and your experience. Only an experienced sales person would be able to present so convincingly and if you really seem to know your stuff they are considering signing you on. The tip off is that this question comes at the wrong time, in the wrong part of your presentation. This question belongs right up front at the beginning but here it is, lying out there in the middle of your presentation, just as you were reaching the most important and juicy part of your pitch.

See what I mean about the question being actually more than it might appear?

Now if you didn't realize that the client was asking for a resume of your experience you would probably respond briefly and succinctly. Most sales people would answer the question with a number

> *" I've been selling (6 years, or 2 years or 20 years)"*

But through SMART SELLING we realize that the answer to: *"How long have you been selling widgets?"* isn't a number . . . it's an explanation. As we have seen any time the client asks for more information use that opportunity to make your case stronger. You are selling from the minute you walk in the door but you must do it with a light touch and subtly.

> *" I started with GIZMO back in 2004 but I've been selling widgets for a number of years before that. GIZMO made me a terrific offer to represent their products when they changed lines to this new model. That was nearly six years ago and in that short space of time we really grabbed a large share of the market with the new 101 design."*

Indirectly we are telling the buyer that not only do we have lots of experience, GIZMO felt so impressed with our experience that they made a special offer to get us involved with this new improved model.

But that's not all. We also got across the idea that, GIZMO is aggressive and constantly looking for ways to increase their market share. That means they are constantly improving the product. And lastly, the new design of the model 101 must have solved lots of problems because it did the trick and increased market share.

That's a lot of ground covered with a simple answer to a simple question. But the key was to recognize what the client was actually asking for. Compare this manner of answer with the usual salesman's. Instead of saying *"6 years"* we've moved way beyond the question and built up Gizmo's image as an aggressive firm with a popular design that is well received by customers.

Now the facts of this example aren't very important. What I'd like you to notice is how every statement the salesman makes is aimed at subtly raising the client's comfort level, while still being responsive to the question. This is fundamental to the SMART SELLING approach.

So the words your client uses are important but also pay attention to the timing. The 'When' can have real significance.

Questions that come at the wrong place mean something. That "something" is often critical to the sale. But you have to have your ears open to hear it when it happens. Generally it will stick out in some way because they will signal to you that it's coming. It's a lot like a catcher signaling to a pitcher in a baseball game.

"All right ... here comes the fast ball. BE READY."

Knowing that this form exists gives you the inside track on understanding what your client is actually looking for. It allows you to be responsive to their questions before they even ask them.

Remember these signals are unconscious. They aren't even aware they are sending and they certainly aren't aware that you are receiving. It allows you to look very much on top of the situation. Just between you and me . . . we know you're not reading their mind . . . but to them you're going to look like a regular Houdini.

Emotionally things we discover for ourselves are more believable than things someone else tells us. SMART SELLING allows the customer to make up his or her own mind about the validity of the information. They ask a question. We answer not only that question but we add a bit more. They then ask another question and since they are asking the questions they will evaluate each answer at their own pace. But since we are always adding more information we are constantly molding the image that they have of the product and of the company. We are managing their mental image of our company and the product and moving them toward a close.

It is critical that we answer ever question however. If they ask us *"What is your return policy"* and we go on and on about how reliable the equipment is and don't mention the return policy, we seem to be dodging the question. But to establish your credibility you have to give a direct answer to every question. Then you can add a little bit of information beyond what they asked to keep the momentum.

Here's another situation, which needs some thought.

You are presenting and suddenly they ask:

"Do you have a return policy?"

Your first reaction might be: *"Really now can this be a serious question?"* Of course GIZMO has a return policy. Every company in the WIDGET biz has a return policy. So they know that you have a return policy. So what are they really asking for?

Should you just say. *"YES, we do."* Think about this from the SMART SELLING point of view. How do you handle this?

A question with such an obvious answer is going to be more than it seems. So what is REALLY bothering the client? To find out what is behind this seemingly "dumb" question don't be afraid to take it head on. Go ahead and ask them:

"Why do you ask?"

At this point the follow up will appear.

"Well I was wondering how long I could use this before making up my mind."

So the question they asked isn't really *"Do you have a return policy?,"* the question is actually *"Can I try this out?"* Not exactly a dumb question is it? But it also isn't the kind of thing a client would feel comfortable asking right at the beginning of a conversation. A try out indicates sincere interest and they don't want to tip their hand quite yet. They want some elbowroom.

OK so what do you do with:

> "Well I was wondering how long I could use this before making up my mind."

The standard sales person response would probably be: "We have a 30 day return policy." That's directly responsive to the question but since you now realize that that is not exactly what the client wants to know, you would look a little deeper, behind the actual words to what the client is signaling. Doesn't the client want to know if they can try it out? They aren't looking for a number; they're looking for permission.

So give them permission and show that you are on their side. After all you want them to look upon you as a consultant, as a reliable counselor. You aren't selling them widgets; you're advising them on improving their business. Of course the Model 101 WIDGET just happens to be one of the ways they can improve their business. . A possible answer to this question might be :

> " We want you to feel comfortable with our product. Did you know we have a one-hour DVD training course that will familiarize you with all of the functions of the model 101 and that it's absolutely free? You can use it right at

Start Selling Smart!

home at your own pace. If at the end of the training, you don't feel the product is right for you, just pack it up and ship it back."

Notice that this answer seems to offer UNLIMITED time to return it but the truth is it's an offer that probably will never be taken up. If after a month and a half they want to send the unit back GIZMO would still take it back. You don't want unhappy customers no matter how long they use the equipment. But chances are that after a month and a half, they will keep the unit even if they don't like it. By then it will be too embarrassing to ship it back (especially if they haven't bothered to take the training). If they do ship it back you can follow up with a phone call and ask why? What didn't you like? How can we improve? It might be a lost sale but at least you'll get some valuable information, which will help you in the future.

We are answering the buyer's question... *Do you have a return policy?* We just aren't curtly cutting them off with "*30 days."* The truth is there actually isn't a real hard deadline. "*Buy it... if you don't like it send it back."*

Why set up an artificial barrier when in truth the company probably wouldn't enforce it anyway?

Instead we continued to sell...

"We have a training program. Won't cost you a cent. We want you to be happy. We want you to feel comfortable with our product."

Now THAT'S exactly what the client wants. They want to be comfortable with the product. You have agreement not a war.

This procedure of carefully considering each question that your client asks can yield big benefits. It will place your presentation ahead of the standard sales pitch because you are so "responsive". You seem to understand intuitively what they need and want. Who wouldn't want to deal with such an insightful salesperson?

So far we've analyzed several ways to squeeze information out of the words and questions your client might use. We've seen how the timing of their questions can give us an insight into what they are thinking.

Let's now move on to the most important part of the presentation...The end.

OK, let's say you've gotten to the end of your pitch. They have listened to your presentation. At the end they lean back and say:

"Well let me think this over and I'll get back to you."

And they take the materials you brought with you and stack them neatly in their out box. What do you think? Did you make the sale or not?

My guess is that you didn't make the sale. Why? Well by stacking your presentation AND PUTTING IT IN THEIR OUT BOX they are signaling that they feel they have given this matter all the time it deserves and that it can be put away. They are dismissing it from their mind. While they might be saying

> "Well let me think this over and I'll get back to you."

The truth is they have already decided and you and your product have been filed away.

However if they had said: *"Let me keep this presentation and show it to my boss."* And then if they had taken the materials you brought with you and stacked them neatly, kept them in their hands and didn't file them away; I would give it a different interpretation.

The stacking in conjunction with the words *"show it to my boss"* means they WILL present this to their boss and they want to make sure they have all the facts and that they are in an organized form.

Notice in the second example they aren't taking the materials from you. They are asking for your permission. (*"Let me keep this presentation . . ."*) Now you don't ask for permission from someone who isn't going to be around. So they must think you might be around.

If they had said: *"I'd like to keep this artwork, do you mind?"* and leave it on the desk where you had put it and tap on it. What would that mean?

Since they probably don't collect artwork for a display at home, they aren't sure what they want to do with it. They might take it forward or they might not. That's why the question *"Do you mind?"* Just in case your product makes the cut.

But what if they had said:" *I'd like to keep this artwork, do you mind?"* and then put it in their briefcase?

I'd guess they probably aren't going to take it forward but there's something about it that they want to show to someone (though it probably isn't the boss). The briefcase is the tip off. They are going to take that art somewhere else and it isn't next door or down the corridor to the boss. They are "hiding" it in their brief case. So something else is afoot here.

Let's say you are in a conference room and you've been making your presentation and the SR VP of Sales interrupts you and says: *"Say could I see that artwork?"* You know you have them intrigued not by what you said but by something he or she likes about the way it looks. Now depending on the product this can vary. But the fact that the SR VP of Sales wants to hold a piece of your presentation means they like something and want to consider how it will look as part of their line. They are imagining that they had it to present. This also can mean that they are accepting (quite literally) what you are saying.

Let's review what we just learned.

Clients often will say things and do it so indirectly that the information they are seeking could get lost if you're not on your toes. Most salespeople would be lost by the question and flummoxed by how to handle it.

But not you.

Watch out for questions that seem to have obvious answers. They generally give you the clue that there's something more going on than immediately meets the eye. But in order to get at the something else you have to be sensitive to what the client is thinking and what they need to know.

These questions are generally ones with an obvious answer that are often couched as a question asking for an OPINION. *"Isn't that an awful lot?"* . Questions like that aren't supposed to be answered with a *'yes'* or a *'no.'* The client is asking for an opinion and you need to respond with an opinion and more information.

Watch out for questions that are out of place. You are talking about the widget and they ask about you. "*How long have you been with GIZMO?"* They are trying to get more information about you and the company. They don't give a hoot if you've been with GIZMO 16 years or 6 years. They want to know about who's standing behind this and with what are they standing.

All presentations follow a natural order. Who, what, why, when, where and generally end with HOW MUCH. If they jump ahead this is signaling that you are making good headway and that they are willing to dispense with some of the steps. Obviously, if the customer is familiar with you or your product line then a lot of the initial waltzing about will be cut short. Why go over the same territory twice? But once they start to talk, start listening.

The moment they quit asking about the product or about your company or your qualifications and begin to talk about themselves or their way of doing business. SHUT UP AND PAY ATTENTION. It means they are starting to think about how you and your product will interface with other departments.

Just like the question about price we discussed above, this is a very important step. There is no reason to concern themselves with your interaction with anyone else in their company if you aren't going to be sticking around, is there? So if they ask:

Start Selling Smart!

"Have you ever worked with Speakup, Tellum and Listen, our advertising agency?"

"Are you familiar with our contractor Biggum, Bigger and Big?"

You know that at least someone in the room is thinking of bringing you aboard. This means you are getting closer to a sale.

SMART SELLING

WHEN THEY QUIT ASKING ABOUT YOUR PRODUCT OR YOU OR YOUR COMPANY AND TALK ABOUT THEMSELVES.

STOP TALKING AND START LISTENING

He or she wants to find a way to make this work. They want you to work with them as a team. So this simple change of topic is a big signal that things are working out nicely for you, widget-wise. And notice it isn't what they are saying so much as what stands directly behind what they are saying. Looking behind the words is SMART SELLING and critical to making the sale.

CHAPTER SEVEN

GESTURES

Human communication doesn't just rely on words. We gesture in certain ways to communicate the way we actually fee as well. So there are actually two different conversations going on at the same time. One is the typical one you would expect which is you and the buyer talking to each other. The other is a silent interchange between you and your buyer that takes place in a code that both of you understand, but that you might not be taking as seriously as you should. It's easy to disregard this information because it is subtle and you've got lots on your mind. But you do so at your peril.

That second conversation is the key in understanding if you are going to make this sale. Making you aware of that second language is what the SMART SELLING technique is built upon.

Here's a simple example:

If we don't want someone else to know our true feelings, we will say one thing with words and indicate something entirely different with a gesture. How many times have you seen this:

Let's say there are three people in a conversation. One is a complete jerk. He's saying something really dumb to you. You smile and nod your head as he speaks. But you make eye contact with your friend, who is standing behind the idiot who is droning on. What do you do? You crinkle your eyebrow or roll your eyes the minute you can do so without being seen by the jerk with the big mouth and the empty head. Right? Now you might very well have said:

"Ohhh sure. Certainly. I completely agree"

But that doesn't really reflect the way you feel. And you want to tell your friend NOT to believe you. You want to communicate something entirely different, actually just the opposite of what you have said. So when you can, you roll your eyes around. Have you ever done that? Have you ever seen that? Sure you have. EVERYONE has.

But think about it. Why do something so strange as rolling your eyes around? It's a way of communicating that is completely non verbal but wow it sure speaks loudly doesn't it?

But did you realize that you would roll your eyes even if no one else were there?

WHAT? Why would someone roll his eyes if there were no one else to see it?

It's an unconscious response. It might be very subtle, but it's done because you are talking to yourself and telling yourself that YOU don't believe a word of it.

I'll bet you've done it from time to time, yourself, especially when you are talking to some idiot on the telephone. Instead of laughing at them and insulting them, you roll your eyes and say to yourself:

> *"I can't believe this guy is this dumb"*

Here you are, all by yourself. No one can see you, yet, you roll your eyes or shake your head in disbelief. Well who are you talking to? Why are you shaking your head?

You can't help it. You're hard wired to react this way. AND THAT is what SMART SELLING counts on. We say one thing with words and another with a gesture to communicate MORE than just the words alone. This holds true no matter where we are or what we are doing. It's inbuilt. It's the way we communicate. The only real difference between spoken words and this other way of communicating (and this is important and worth remembering) is that words are consciously selected and gestures are completely unconscious. Unconscious means uncensored. It means truthful. Why?

When we talk to each other two different things are going on simultaneously. We are talking with words but were also talking with gestures. The words we speak reflect the logical part of our feeling, the gestures and moves we make reflect the emotional side. We combine them to get the idea across

Let's talk about the logical side first. Talking is actually thinking out loud. And when we speak we take care in how we say something. We try to accurately describe what we are thinking. We choose our words carefully and we have a lot of words to pick from.

I've heard it said that the Eskimos have a variety of different words in their language for the word "snow." We don't. Why the difference? In the North where there is a lot of snow, the kind of snow can make the difference between life and death. There's the kind of snow that lies over thin ice and the kind that contains very little water, there's a kind of snow that falls before a large storm and so forth. If you don't live at the North Pole or speak Eskimo you don't need many words to describe snow because you actually couldn't care less about the kind of snow it is. To you it's just the white, wet stuff that makes driving tricky and Christmas pretty. So you and I think about snow in a different way than Eskimos do.

Our language is made up of thousands of words, which express all these nuances of thought. We pick through these words very carefully when we speak. It's a very careful and logical process that is ENTIRELY conscious.

We don't say " *That was an unusual presentation"* when what we actually mean is *"That was a unique presentation."* If you go to the dictionary the words "unusual" and "unique" can be very close in meaning but when we use them with certain other words they take on an entirely different meaning. Often this is a subtle difference but we know it is and that's why we consciously picked that particular word. We consciously choose the word to most accurately describe what we're thinking. Speaking is conscious thinking.

But we also express ourselves in even finer and subtler ways than with words alone,. To do that we ADD something to what we say to make our feelings even clearer. We generally do it with a gesture.

What if we crinkled our eyebrow when we said: *"That was a unique presentation"?* Aren't we actually casting doubt on the presentation itself? Aren't we being ironic? We are saying that the presentation was unique in an odd way. We are communicating that we feel the presentation was oddly unusual not outstandingly unusual.

If we crinkle our eyebrow we're communicating our emotional feeling. We're adding to our words an emotional component. There is no other way to communicate this feeling. That crinkle is critical to get the tone of what we are thinking across. That crinkle is just as important to the idea as the words are. It's a way of communicating with words and telling the recipient how we feel at the same time.

AND WE DO THIS ALL THE TIME.

It's as if we speak two languages at the same time, one logical delivered in words and one emotional and delivered in gestures and expressions. The combination of the two can be very revealing.

When you observe what the client is saying and combine that with what the client is doing as he speaks, you begin to see that there is more going on behind the words than you might have thought AND the way your client puts those words together can give you an amazing amount of information as well. Selling Smart uses the non-verbal part to grasp what the client feels. We are so used to speaking with gestures to enhance what we speak that we are unaware of it. The gestures are inbuilt. Unconscious.

This is GOOD for you!

That's the edge you can have if you pay attention to what your client is doing, what your client is saying and observe how your client behaves in a meeting. I call that "reading the room." If you pay attention and change your pitch in subtle ways as you read the room, you'll find that you're selling becomes a lot easier. You'll close more sales and win more clients.

Start Selling Smart!

The nice part about SMART SELLING is that you don't have to be an anthropologist to read the gestures and rituals hard wired into our communication, BECAUSE YOU USE THEM ALL THE TIME reading the client is going to be easy. As an example:

When someone does a really good job what do we instinctively do? We pat them on the back. LITERALLY. We actual strike them on the shoulder or back. Now we aren't angry are we? We aren't actually striking them to hurt them are we? No, we are congratulating them. It's almost an uncontrollable instinct.

When we see someone for the first time in a day what do we do? We wave our hand and say:" *HI*," don't we? Why would we do something so silly? What purpose does it serve? I've heard anthropologists add that we raise our hand to make ourselves more visible.

Well really now, if you're nearly 6 feet tall how will raising your hand make you more visible? It won't. So what do we do. . . . we wave our hand. The movement is to catch the eye.

Before you reject this as a lot of baloney consider this. Why is it that we only shake hands the first time we greet someone in a day BUT NOT THE SECOND TIME. Well WHY? If it was just a meaningless gesture to wave our hand and smile and say: "*Hi*" the first time we saw them then why NOT do it every time?

The answer an anthropologist might give is that we have already communicated what we needed to

> *" I see you and I recognize you"*

So the next time we see them that day we KNOW the other person has already made that statement. WE HAVE ALREADY HAD THAT DISCUSSION so to speak. But we actually didn't say anything.

NOW THIS IS IMPORTANT.

The gesture tells us what the person is thinking, even though they didn't SAY much at all. As a matter of fact we don't have to say "*Hi*" at all and STILL the idea gets across.

We use ritual gestures like this all the time. They are a short hand way of communicating. We use them so often that we often don't realize how revealing they can be. If you pay attention it's amazing how many rituals we use in business. And they can tell you a lot.

These rituals and gestures must be there to complete any deal. BUT what if a big deal is signed and everyone is happy but one person. What if one person doesn't smile and laugh? We know something is amiss. This is just like NOT saying *"Hi"* and waving your hand.

Trouble.... big trouble is coming.

Start Selling Smart! 99

The way a client acts often will tell you more than what he says because it reveals what he feels. And feeling is a lot more important than talking or thinking. No customer is going to buy something that makes him or her feel uneasy. So if he or she signs and stomps out of the room, they have told you a lot without saying a word.

So what kinds of gestures should you be looking out for?

This is where close observation is required. We are so used to seeing these that it often doesn't register in our minds what we have just seen. It's as if someone waved at us from across the room. We wave back and in a flash forget it. But SMART SELLING requires that we note the unconscious movements others make and read it in the context of the moment. What did they do and say when they did this movement.

To give you an idea of the kinds of things to look for here are a few examples. Lets say you are pitching and

1. They blink at what you said. What does it mean?

You've just told them something they didn't expect. *"Wow what a surprise."* This may mean that you are making real headway and you might want to continue down that path. It depends of course on what is was that you were saying. It may be that you are losing them and they are surprised at what you said because clearly it wasn't what they thought you were going to say. So if they appear annoyed you would want to stop this line of approach.

2.If they glance at someone else and nod their head they are passing along what you just said to that other person. It is often a *"See I told you so"* gesture. They are taking what you said and carrying it on to the person they glanced at.

3.If they glance down they don't like what they are hearing and probably are rejecting what you are saying. It's an avoidance reaction, which means you are losing ground on this point. It's as if they were throwing your point to the ground.

4.If they look down and away, they are thinking something negative about what you are saying. They are concerned that you might read it in their eyes so they are breaking eye contact with you. They need to be "alone" for a moment to think about it.

5.If they look at you they are signaling either agreement or interest. *"Yeah . . . tell me more"* This means you should continue down this path and keep making similar points. They are listening and agreeing.

6.If they look at you while you are talking with both eyes wide open they are surprised and impressed. You are saying something that is having a big impact. But be careful... that impact might be negative or positive. It really depends upon what you were saying at the time.

If you determine it is positive then follow up with additional points along a similar line. Use the gesture, as a way to determine which direction the presentation should go. You have found a "hot button" so for goodness sake, don't let go of it.

7. If they look away while you are talking and keep both eyes wide open, they are talking to themselves. They are trying to convince themselves of something by talking it out. I find it's generally best to let them puzzle it out for themselves and add information if I can be helpful. There may be something confusing them and they need time to absorb what you have just said.

SO PAUSE.

Let the client catch up. This is where the traditional sales approach fails. Most sales people would keep on punching when in fact there is no need to and pressure at this point might actually hurt the sale.

8. If they roll their eyes while you are talking . . . they didn't believe you. Need I add this is not a good sign? You need to take this signal very seriously. It means you have skipped some important fact and that isn't sitting very well. STOP. Ask them what is upsetting to them or what is it that bothers them. Get it out on the table pronto. If you miss this opportunity to nail down this problem it will kill your sale for sure.

Now you might ask:

"How do I know when the gesture is a really significant one and when it's not. What if the guy has something in his eye? What if his nose itches? What if he isn't glancing at someone he's just staring out the window.?"

All gestures don't always mean something obviously. You have to look out for certain gestures IN CERTAIN PLACES. Nothing happens in isolation.

Your meeting or presentation doesn't take place as a series of snap shots. One thing follows another, there's a flow to everything. So you must be aware of what is happening as you are saying something and after you have said it.

You make these observations as the meeting flows along. . Your focus should be on the client not on you. Notice how what you say affects what they do. That's the clue. Then notice what they do as they speak. That communicates as well.

Earlier we discussed how the typical sales person concentrates on THEIR presentation, on THEIR product, on THEIR meeting. This is a bad habit you will need to take in hand. It will probably be the most difficult part of learning SMART SELLING.

You have to give up the idea that you are important to the process. It isn't about what you do or say. It's about what they do and say. Not only that but it's also about what they do and say when you do or say something. In short it's how they respond.

When we put all these gestures together they begin to tell a story. It's as if there were a subtitle running under what they say. That subtitle reveals what they are thinking as you speak or as they respond. It gives you guidance, which you can't get any other way. Here's an example:

Let's say that you're in a meeting and the VP of Distribution is really worried about how poorly his department has performed in the past. He needs to get some reassurance. Here's how he might do it and here's how SMART SELLING can save your sale.

Let's say he asks:

"Now aren't these parts going to be hard to get?"

and glances over at his boss and then immediately thereafter asks:

"Where are your distribution centers?"

What do you imagine it means? They seem like pretty straightforward questions, right? Why any person in distribution would want to know that, wouldn't they?

So how do you know that the clowns in distribution are a disaster?

This is where you read your customer. By observing that little flicker of an eye movement over to his boss you know that George has had a problem like this before and his boss knows it. So aren't you going to look like a genius when you say:

> "You know, George, one of the things the guys in distribution are going to like is our overnight parts delivery. We've been able to service clients as far away as Nova Scotia the same afternoon they needed the parts."

Bingo, you have just hit a home run. George's eyes will light up like a kid at Christmas and he'll break out into a big grin. His whole face will relax. What a relief. George will be absolutely stunned. You just took down the really big hang up that was making George so nervous.

BUT . . . how did we know that was exactly what he wanted to hear? Did he have a little meeting with you before the meeting and whisper it in your ear?

Of course not. You used SMART SELLING. You noticed his gestures, his eyes, and mainly what he didn't say to tell you what was on his mind. He indicated it in the way he asked questions and you listened. Let's go over this seemingly simple encounter and take it apart piece by piece.

If George said:

"Now aren't these parts going to be hard to get?"

and he glances over at his boss what is he really saying?

First let's look at the logic of the situation. Isn't it obvious? He already knows how you are going to answer because the question is a loaded one.

Notice the question...*are the parts going to be easy to get?* I'd say the answer was pretty obvious, wouldn't you? OF COURSE you are going to say that your parts are easy to get.

You'd be crazy to say to him:

"Gee George that's the one flaw with our product... the parts are really hard to come by. It's a real big problem"

So George really DOESN'T want you to tell him that the parts are easy to get, so he is actually asking something different. What? What kind of game is George playing and why is it important?

This seemingly innocent question is a tip off to a problem. People don't ask questions that they already know the answer too. So he's purposely sending a signal. It's what he isn't saying that is important not what he is saying. Why would someone ask a really inappropriate question, one that everyone in the room already knows the answer to? Obviously George doesn't expect the obvious answer.

THAT'S YOUR TIP OFF.

George is looking for something else isn't he? There must be something behind that simple question and it means we need to look behind the words for the real problem. It's what he says next that will tell you.

If he immediately asks,

"Where are your distribution centers?"

and glances at his boss. It becomes clear. It tells you that George is really WORRIED about distribution, his area. He's had a problem with distribution center location before AND HIS BOSS KNOWS IT.

That's why he glanced at his boss. He made eye contact for a reason. He's passing the question along and emphasizing it to his boss. That means this area is sensitive. Something has happened before where the location of distribution centers was important. YOU KNOW THAT and not a single word was spoken telling you that. You watched and you listened.

Let's look at what we know:

George is worried about how his department is going to look. George is worried about what his boss will think IF he has a problem. George is wondering how big a

Start Selling Smart!

problem your wonderful widget is going to be. He's had a problem with distribution before. He's telling you he has a problem (and hasn't said a word to you about it).

He's thinking:

> *"If these parts are hard to find, the clowns in my department aren't going to know how to handle this. None of them have any initiative. They'll panic. I'm going to have to sit on this baby like a bull rider in a rodeo with a rope between my teeth."*

When George says:

> *"Where are your distribution centers?"*

and glances at his boss, he's communicating something other than curiosity about the location of your distribution centers. He's saying:

> *"If they don't have a distribution center near me, I'm going to be sitting there with a three day lag time and the boss is going to skin me alive, just like he did with the Phillips order last week. I need to show my boss that I won't get sandbagged by a company that can't service us, because they don't have a nearby distribution center.*
>
> *SO I'M GOING TO NAIL THIS DOWN RIGHT NOW.*
>
> *I'm going to signal my boss that I KNOW this has been a problem and I want him to realize that I'm on top of it.* So

I'll look over at him to make sure he's paying attention to what I am saying. Once I've done that he'll know that I'm on top of this. Man oh man I can't screw up again Denise just got new braces. I NEED THIS JOB."

But do you realize that most sales people who didn't use SMART SELLING would never pick up on this sensitivity?

Most salespeople would just answer the questions in a straightforward way and not give it a second thought. Notice that the salesperson might as well be fast asleep because they are missing more than half of what is actually being said.

"Now aren't these parts going to be hard to get?"

Is answered by

"No, our parts are easy to get."

"Where are your distribution centers?"

is answered by

"We have several distribution centers all around the Midwest."

Now isn't that just great? The client asked two questions and the salesman gave two answers. WONDERFUL. They answered the wrong question by giving the wrong answer and they missed the chance to take down the really serious but unspoken problem that might kill this deal.

It was there, but they missed it.

Did they deal with what was REALLY bothering George? Distribution centers all around the Midwest might be swell but HOW NEAR are they to George and HOW FAST can those centers react? Yet the traditional sales person thinks they answered the question but we can see now that they didn't even come close. Yet the answer was right there if they had only been paying attention.

This was simple!

Everyone knows that when one person glances at another they are checking to see if that person is listening. You do it all the time. This isn't information that's locked up somewhere. You don't have to be Einstein to figure this out. My goodness, you do this every day. So why would anybody miss this obvious little flicker.

The answer as I'm sure you are beginning to realize is one of focus.

Most salespeople are NOT looking at the client. They are looking at their presentation and the slides, at the write up, at the graphs, at just about everything but what they should be looking at . . . the client and their client's reaction to what the sales person is saying. And so you won't be surprised, will you, when this salesperson blows this sale sky high? Frankly they deserve it.

But with SMART SELLING you would KNOW there was something behind those questions because you would read what was going on in your client's head and instead of missing an opportunity you would have said:

> "You know, George, one of the things the guys in distribution are going to like is our overnight parts delivery. We've been able to service clients in Nova Scotia the same afternoon they needed the parts."

Bear in mind that the only reason you are going through all of this is to make George let go of that rope that he thinks is holding him back from buying. Until he lets go you won't make a sale. He must feel comfortable that this restraint is not an issue.

For the good of this sale we can't afford to leave George sitting there worried about this because if he is, he isn't going to be working with you to sell your product! And you need all the help you can get.

As a matter of fact until he's converted to your side, he's your enemy. If he's worried about your potential to make him look bad in front of the boss is he going to look for reasons to urge the company to buy your product?

NO.

Now think about this . . . if he has the slightest creepy feeling that this could turn out like the Phillips deal is he going to stand up and make your case after you left the building?

Hardly!

And if we don't solve this problem it can really get out of hand.

Until he is comfortable that your widget is going to be easy to handle, he will fight it tooth and nail. Your widget is poison. If your widget is poison why on earth will George want to defend it? He won't. He'll do everything in his power to destroy it. And worse than that he'll do it behind your back, in the dark, where you can't fight back. He won't do it now, at this moment, in this meeting. No, he'll do it after you've gone, over the water cooler when the time is right.

You'll be driving back to the office, congratulating yourself on what a great presentation you just made and how terrific the charts and graphs looked and while you are doing that he'll casually mention to his boss.

"You know that Widget worries me, boss. I'm not sure they can deliver what they say they can deliver. Has anyone checked them out? We don't want another repetition of the Phillips deal, DO WE?"

Notice the issue is not your widget. It's a great product and you made a great presentation. He's can't knock a hole in your widget so he'll go after YOU. George will deflect attention to your company, to you, to all kinds of things other than his department. If he can plant enough suspicion about this deal, the boss will kill this. That means George doesn't have to worry about how he will look if the parts are slow or his crew of clowns drops the ball once again.

WHAT! You mean to say that George is THAT selfish. He would actually sabotage something that is good for the company that might make the company a lot of money for such a petty reason. What kind of a team player is this guy, George? He couldn't be that self centered.

But that is just the point. George couldn't care less if your product is going to make his company huge profits and assure its long-term survival in the industry. He is self-centered. He has to be. He's only interested in HIS long-term survival. He's got a life to lead. He's got a golf score and his daughter's braces to worry about. Let the big wigs in the front office worry about the industry. That's what they get paid the big bucks for. He has a job to protect and he isn't about to let your widget wreck it.

That's why every potential problem must be dispatched. If they are still standing when you leave the room you have left a problem behind and they grow. They grow and they grow in the dark where you can't dig them out.

That's where you and your product are vulnerable.
After you leave is when the damage is done. And you can't do a thing about it. SO you must make sure you don't leave any rock unturned. You have got to dig out every possible problem. Your job as a salesperson is to understand their problems and provide the answers. Mainly it's going to be your job to make sure that ever person in that room feels that your widget is going to be good for their company, easy to bring into the company and that your company will help them ALL look good.

Let's say that we are pitching our widget to ACME and you are talking about the price and just as you get to the part about financing you notice the Head of Sales glance at the Head of Marketing and blinks. What happened?

We know that the glance at someone else means they are passing along what you said. So Sales wants Marketing to make note of the price. Then Sales blinked. So what does it mean.? You already know what it means because you know what you do when you blink at what someone says. You're surprised.

If someone says: *"Hey I just heard you got a raise."* And you didn't know anything about it. The first thing you would do before you said a single word would be...blink. Astonishment. WOW.

So you know what that blink means because you use it everyday. This isn't some foreign language that only a few dusty scholars can find in a tomb somewhere. Everybody does this. This is not difficult.

That blink is surprise, isn't it?

Sales and Marketing have discussed this before and Sales thought the price was going to be at a certain number, which Marketing didn't agree with or which Marketing thought would make the purchase difficult. When the price came in the way it did, Marketing wanted to know what Sales thought about it and Sales wanted Marketing to know that they were surprised. So they blinked. This was an entire non-verbal discussion that went on right in front of your face and if you were paying attention revealed a lot about what your customer was thinking.

So far these gestures are pretty simple but did you realize that you could squeeze a little more out of this discussion than knowing that Sales is surprised?

It would, of course, depend upon what you were saying so the meaning can vary. But if you were talking about how inexpensive the product actually would be in operation and Sales liked that, they would want to make sure that Marketing heard that.

So Sales would make eye contact with Marketing and smile. This would make the point that this would be a good item to bring aboard. Do you realize how important that might be? You have an ally in the room.

Sales thinks this is a good item to bring aboard. You are on your way to making a sale! BUT did you catch it or did you ignore it? With SMART SELLING you'd be one up on the usual salesperson that just keeps rolling along like Old Man River.

On the other hand if the price was higher than expected then Sales could be signaling to Marketing that the price was going to be an issue and this was going to be tough to sell at this price point. Sales would look at Marketing to get Marketing's attention and raise an eyebrow or scowl slightly. They might make a tiny shake of the head.

Be careful here. These are not going to be big gestures. They're small. It's sort of a physical version of whispering.

So does that mean your deal is dead and your goose is cooked? Far from it. It means you have a problem that needs to be addressed. So no matter what you were going to say, no matter what was next on your list of sales points STOP.

Deal with the price issue pronto. Don't let it fester and don't let it set up in cement. The longer you delay, the harder it will be to undo. You immediately explain why the price is worth it or how sales at the new price point have actually gone up. This is the time to use whatever you have to take this concern down.

Notice that the more you squeeze on the interpretation the less accurate it becomes. The simple gesture gives you a hint at the problem and perhaps the solution. If you take it a bit farther you accuracy will begin to decline. Like shooting an arrow at a target, the further away the target, the less accurate you can expect to be.

But remember these are just your thoughts and suspicions. They are things you can consider, not necessarily things frozen in stone. They give you a place to start when you analyze your progress. If you come up with two possibly contradictory things, fine. There is a flow to any sale and further down the line more information will come your way, which will tell you where you are. It's a dynamic way to fuel your progress. It changes from moment to moment and day to day.

SMART SELLING takes in this non-verbal information and translates it into an insight into your client's thinking, which you can use. It can reveal who is on your side and who is not. It can reveal where the ice is thin and where you need to reassure. But most importantly it allows you to answer client's questions as they occur to them and before they lead the client away from the purchase.

Using this method you change your presentation as you read the client. They tell you how to conduct the meeting instead of losing control of it because you aren't reading what is going on in the room.

If you are responsive to their concerns you will notice that shortly the room warms up. You seem to have all the answers. Their interest will rise. The tone will gradually change from hostility to a new product, to serous consideration of a helpful item. This is the direction you want the pitch to go. What the client doesn't realize is that they are telling you what they want to hear and you are responding to their direction. They will feel good about this presentation because it will answer the questions that are forming in their head just at the moment they form. Negative thoughts don't get a chance to harden into a set idea. Preconceived ideas aren't allowed to remain uncorrected.

Actually SMART SELLING can do something else which is critical to a sale, especially if it's a customer you don't know very well. SMART SELLING waits for the client to tell you what they are thinking as we have already explained, but did you realize that by waiting for your client to react it also gives you a way to pace the presentation?

As we present it's often easy to forget that our pace of presentation is very important. SMART SELLING will allow you to set the pace of the transaction because it is tied to the client and their speed of reaction to what you are saying or tied to the rate at which they are responding. As they react to your response the pace of the meeting will adjust. This means they are constantly telling you the speed at which they want the presentation to go. SMART SELLING can protect you from pushing too hard or not hard enough.

SMART SELLING allows the client to set the pace but only if you let it. Think of the meeting as a Ouija board. Just a very light touch will guide the meeting toward a conclusion. You must not overpower the client by racing to a close. They will buy when they are darn good and ready and not a second before. So racing to the finish line might make you feel better that the presentation is over but it might ruin your chance of making a sale because you left the client back in the dust cloud.

Our manner of presentation is important too. Everyone deals with things at their own rate. That can be a problem. Some clients need to debate with themselves or with each other before moving on to the next section of your presentation. They will signal when they want you to proceed but you have to be sensitive and look for their signal. Often it will just be a slight nod and a smile after a moment of reflection. This probably means they have digested what you have said and are ready for more. If the client wants to deal in a slow and careful manner, the whole process is going to take longer. One the other hand, sometimes they are following easily and things can move right along. It depends upon them. Which is exactly the way it should be.

With traditional methods of presenting however the pace is always in the hands of the presenter and that might mean that a lot of the presentation goes right over the customer's head. What a waste. It might even have been a decent presentation. Actually by allowing the client to respond as you present you make sure they are paying attention to what you have to say as well as giving you feedback to potential problems as they might occur.

With certain cultures haste is a sign of bad manners. The Japanese are well known for their extremely slow approach to business. They consider the American " *let's get this deal done"* attitude impolite. So directness is tied closely to culture. SMART SELLING can help signal to you which pace is the right one. By watching the client and reacting rather than acting, they tell you how fast or slow to go.

CHAPTER EIGHT

ON THE TELEPHONE

Now that you have the principles of SMART SELLING in hand let's see SMART SELLING in action from the very first prospecting telephone call you make to set up the meeting through the presentation and finally to the follow up call to see if you made the sale or not.

The first contact with the client is important because it determines what kind of an impression the client will have about you and your product and it gives you an idea of whom you are dealing with. You do that by SMART SELLING right from the moment you pick up the phone.

At first glance it might seem that picking a client would be the least of the problems you would have to overcome in selling your widget. But any sale requires someone to buy it and if we pick our entry point carefully our job will be much easier.

Let's say you have a list of potential clients. To sell the product you need to be smart about the way you approach each client on that list. Believe it or not companies are a lot like people, they have body language and gestures and the combination, if read correctly, can reveal mountains of information. The body language of the company is the way the building looks and the furniture in the reception room, the office, the conference room. The words that a company has are it's receptionist, it's switchboard the way they deal with the outside. It's what they "say" to the outside by the way they act and look. Let's deal with the words first and see how much we can squeeze out of a seemingly simple phone call.

Our first task is to get in the door and it's not just any door either. We want to get into the right door and we want to prepare our way in, so that our client is preconditioned even before we meet with them to think positively about our widget system. Well how do we know which entry point to pick?

There is ONE person who knows all this.

The first person in the company who always gets the call . . . the switchboard operator.

If it's a large company, it will have a switchboard. Often I find that the most helpful person in a company is that switchboard operator. After all, this employee is familiar with all the key people in the company. The switchboard operator knows who's busy and who's not. The operator will have a company directory right on his or her desk.

That means you want:

1. The right department.
2. The decision-maker in that department.
3. That person's first and last name.
4. That person's title.

The switchboard operator can give you all that, but he or she can give you more if you're clever. Here's how to get:

5. The name of that person's boss.
6. The names of those under him or her.
7. A rough idea of the structure of the entire company.

The ideal case is when you get someone on the switchboard, who has been around a long time. They know everyone and have an opinion about everyone. Those opinions can give you an insight into who is who and what is what. To get at that secret information (and it IS secret) you have to listen for pauses and inflection in the operator's voice. People they like will be referred to in a different way than people they don't like. The operator's voice will rise when they like someone. It's the nonverbal equivalent of *"OH THAT'S A GOOD CHOICE."* They can't say *"Oh that's a good choice"* of course. They will express it in a light tone with a happy lilt to their voice. As you might imagine, this is difficult for me to put onto paper because it depends upon the way the words are said and the rhythm and lilt to their voice. But it will be equivalent to:

"Mr. Smiths Office (and boy am I glad to be here)" rather than

"Mr. Smiths Office (and ugh I really can't stand that dummy)."

But how do you know if the operator is an old hand and knows everyone.? There's a simple test. You ask a question that demands an answer. Such as:

"Who's the Director of Procurement?" instead of *"I'd like the Director of Procurement."*

Why ask a question?

Because now they are going to have to answer the question. AND THAT'S HOW YOU TELL.

It's the speed with which they answer your request. If they fire back the answer in a flash:

> *"Mr. Smith is the Director of Procurement.*
>
> *I'll put you through"*

Viola! ...they know their way around.

If they pause and stumble a bit . . . it signifies that they aren't sure. They probably will qualify what ever they say with *"I think"* or *"I suppose."* It would sound like this:

> *"Uhhh, I think that would be Mr. Smith.*
>
> *Should I put you through?"*

Now in this example, the operator is unconsciously telling you they aren't really sure. They want you to make the decision for them. "Should I put you through?" is asking you to decide because they don't feel qualified. That's the tip off that either they are new or they rarely get asked this question.

Why is this important? You need to determine how reliable the switchboard operator is by finding out how long they've been there. That tells you how much weight to give to their response or to their change in voice inflection.

But you can pickup something else that has value from the operator. If they don't know who the Director of Procurement is, it means that the operator hasn't been asked this very often. AND that tells you that the company and Mr. Smith in particular don't ordinarily get many calls. Both of these things are good to know AND notice NO ONE asked these questions and no one even realized they answered them. But the information was there all the time.

All right, let's say that the operator knows their way around. Here's how I would handle the rest of the conversation to get at the critical information regarding company structure

Operator:

> "Acme Corporation...
>
> How can I direct your call?"

Me:

> "Operator, I have a new communications system I'd like to present to your company and I don't know who to contact. Can you help me?"

Operator: (quickly)

 "That would be Mr. Sheppard in Engineering. I'll connect you."

(She's an old hand isn't she? I can rely on her information)

Don't let her connect you yet!

You need a little more information that she can give you, so I often say something like:

"Just a minute. Do you have a Director of Procurement or a purchasing department?

If a company is large enough to have either a Director of Procurement or a purchasing department, the guys in engineering will be the last people you want to talk to. Why? Because the guys in engineering are the ones who are going to have to install your widget system not buy it. You represent just one more problem they will have to solve, and they don't get paid by the problem. Engineers view their job as finding the most efficient and effective way to use their equipment and make sure the product is going to work. They have only one reason to take on a new project:

They are told to by upper-management.

So you need a meeting with upper-management before you talk about which nut and which bolt goes into your widget. Now did you notice that if you had just picked up the phone with the objective of getting a meeting with anybody, you might have accepted Mr. Sheppard and that would be the wrong person? But, by being a bit more forceful, at this point, you not only will get to the right person, you can also start on your way to a smart sale. Here's how:

Operator:

> "Yes, that would be Mr. Smith. May I connect you?"

Me:

> "Yes, thank you. By the way, what is Mr. Smith's first name?"

Operator:

> "Bill . . . Bill Smith is the Director of Procurement."

Me:

> "Is he a vice president of the company?"

Operator:

> "Why no, that would be Ms. Simpson. She is the VP of Operations. Mr. Smith reports to her."

Before you let this very helpful switchboard operator go, there is another important piece of information, which is ours for the asking-Smith's boss's first name. It'll be handy later.

Me:

> "May I have Ms. Simpson's first name please?"

Operator:

> *"Alice. Ms. Alice Simpson is the VP of Operations.*
>
> *Should I connect you with her office?"*

Now you have the first and last names and the titles of the key players. You also have the beginning of an idea of the structure of the company. If you're really lucky (and attentive) you might also get an idea of how this particular operator feels about Mr. Smith and Ms. Simpson. They might be stinkers or really nice folks. One person's opinion is not enough to build a sales presentation on, but it is a helpful insight into office politics. If you make a mental note of it, when you actually meet these people, it can help you form an opinion of who is the decision maker and who is not.

You will notice as we go through this sales call, that little bits of information will be accumulated that can be cross checked with each other to add validity to the picture we are developing. Now a person's position and title does not necessarily mean that they have the power or the interest to pass judgment on your product. Smith might be just as important an ally as Simpson. For all you know, Simpson may not get involved with something like your product. It's not the title, it's the power to say *"YES"* and make it stick that is important here.

So which will it be Simpson or Smith? This is a judgment call that can go either way. But remember this... if you are the least bit unsure of yourself if you go to Smith's superior and get turned down you are finished, kaput. You can't take it higher you've already blown it. On the other hand, if you get Smith and he can't make a decision you won't make the sale until he clears it with Simpson but you are still in the game.

If you're unsure, go to the lower tier. The chances are that you will do the least amount of damage if the call doesn't go well and you can still remedy the situation. If it seems like a lot of work, I can assure you it isn't. This is all new to you and unexpected. Once you do it a few times, it becomes automatic. You process this quickly and plug it in where you need it. It goes somewhere in your head and makes up your gut feel of the place. By the end of the meeting it will be part of your entire gut feel about the meeting. That gut feel will tell you how you are doing and where you stand.

Now we can let the operator put us through to Bill Smith, but before we talk with any executive, we need to realize that we wouldn't go into any meeting without preparation before hand. That's true of the first phone call too. We must prepare ourselves. Before making a call to a company, memorize a voicemail message to leave behind.

What I mean is a short mini-pitch to place on voicemail if your contact is out of the office. I find that people aren't regularly in the office anymore. Email and voicemail and the Internet make offices a bit obsolete. So you have to have something prepared in advance.

Now the switchboard is putting you through to Bill Smith's office.

Secretary:

> *"Mr. Smith's office. May I help you?"*

Me:

> *"Is Bill available?"*

"(Remember, you got his first name just moments ago.)

Secretary:

> *"I'll check. Does he know what this is regarding?"*

Me:

> *"Tell him I represent a product that will improve the efficiency of his company by 50% and I'd like to show it to him."*

Note I didn't ask for a big meeting. I want Bill to decide if he needs a meeting. A meeting means getting lots of folks involved. And that can tell me something I want to know. If he wants a meeting to meet with outside players, it can tell me a lot about:

1. The need they have for this product.

2. The different departments this is going to involve.

3. How much power Bill actually has to say *"Yes."*

So now Bill Smith has to make a decision. He can stonewall and take a chance that I'm just bluffing. (In which case he'll say he's not in even if he is.).

On the other hand, if I have something that really is that good, and he puts me off, he's going to have egg all over his face.

Secretary:

> *"May I have your name please and I'll see if he's available."*

I give her my name and wait. If he's unavailable I'll be directed to his voicemail.

Let's say I get the voicemail (a typical scenario). This is where the brief memorized pitch comes in. Look at this 30 second memorized message as a mini-meeting. You must grab his attention and get him to set up a meeting. You want to control the sale, so you don't want to just leave your name and number. Often sales people make the mistake of doing exactly what the taped message says, which is something like:

> *"Leave your name and phone number and a brief message and I'll get back to you as soon as I can."*

Don't Do It!

SMART SELLING.

ALWAYS KEEP THE INITIATIVE

This sale is yours to make or lose. If you wait for him to call, you'll be waiting indefinitely. It can be pretty nerve-wracking. He might just stonewall you and you'll never get to him. However, if you keep the initiative, you control the progress of this entire process. Always say in your rehearsed message that you will call back at such and such a time, and leave your email address. Have him agree via email to your suggested time or to another time that he might like better.

So, the pitch goes something like:

> *"Hi, Bill. Sorry I missed you. My name is [your name] and I have a product that has proven to greatly increase the effectiveness of your staff. I think your firm should take a look at this. Why don't I call back on Tuesday at 10? If that's not acceptable, just contact me at (email address) and let me know what time I should call."*

Either he will or he won't respond to your message via email. If he does, you know he's a little intrigued. If he doesn't, you still have the initiative to contact him Tuesday at 10 or whenever you suggested. Now he might decline the 10 a.m. call, but chances are he'll give you an alternate time. This means that he can't stonewall you as easily. It doesn't guarantee he will see you but it does help you get in the door.

But what if he's in his office and take's your call when the secretary transfers you? Well, you have your pitch in place, right?

Now at this point most sales people would move right in with something like this:

> "Hi, Bill. My name is (your name) and I represent the GIZMO Company.
>
> We've put together a new interoffice communications system that actually increases office efficiency by 50%
>
> I think you should take a look at it and I'd like to drop by and show it to you."

Now this is a pretty good opening line. But let's look at it from the SMART SELLING point of view. Bill is a pretty good manager. What you are saying might actually be something he would like to see but he has a lot on his desk. How does he know who GIZMO Co is? As a matter of fact who is this voice on the phone?

Keep in mind the basic Smart Selling maxim:

SMART SELLING

IT'S ALWAYS ABOUT THEM

It's always about what they want, what they need, why they need this, whatever it is that will make them happy. It is NEVER about you. It is never about what you want. It is never about what you need. It is never about whatever it is that will make you happy.

Simple, isn't it?

OK, what possible reason would convince him to waste his valuable time talking with you? What's in it for him?

Notice it is NOT how great your product is. It's what's in it for him or her. What career building is going to be achieved by meeting with you? If you don't have the answer to this . . . don't even make the call. You are just going through the motions. No one will buy your lovely Widget just because you have a list of swell sales points. THEY DON'T CARE.

ALSO...We want to establish a beachhead with our credibility right up front. So we need to trot out our credentials and impress him that he's not wasting his time. We need to give him a reason to see us that is defensible to his boss when the boss says:

Start Selling Smart!

"Bill . . . why did you tie up all that time with that clown from GIZMO when the Jenkins report was needed ASAP?"

So we need to convince Bill that the guys from GIZMO are really something. SMART SELLING means convincing the client that you are worth listening to and worth having around. It means gaining their trust and making the sale a measure of that trust.

From what we have discussed it should be clear that it's you and your company not your product that will give him the feeling that an association with you and your company will make him look good. With that in mind let's redo the opening line to something along these lines:

"Hi, Bill. My name is (your name).

I'm the assistant vice president of domestic sales for the GIZMO Company. You've probably heard of us. We were featured in Business Week last month. We're the folks who helped NASA put the space shuttle into orbit.

Bill, I want to show you something that is really amazing. We've been working with IBM and put together a new interoffice communications system that actually increases office efficiency by 50%. I realize that seems like an incredible number but I can back it up with our research, I'd like to bring it to you so you can judge for yourself. Bill I've been with GIZMO for twenty years and

I've never seen anything as good as this. I think you should take a look at it and I'd like to drop by and show it to you."

Remember earlier when we were selling that 101 Widget and we kept subtly building up our client's confidence in the company by referring to our experience. Well it's just that same here. We want the client to feel good about our company and about our ability to deliver. We want a comfortable tone for all the meetings that follow. So lets read over the opening again and listen as though we were Bill Smith.

"Hi, Bill. My name is (your name). I'm the assistant vice president of domestic sales for the GIZMO company.

(OK this joker is a VP. Hmmmm he might be worth listening too)

You've probably heard of us

(Yeah I think I remember their name*)*

We were featured in Business Week last month

(must be a solid company).

We're the folks who helped NASA put the space shuttle into orbit

(Gee they've done pretty impressive stuff).

Bill, I want to show you something that is really amazing. We've been working with IBM

(hmmm if it's good enough for IBM it must be alright)

and put together a new interoffice communications system that actually increases office efficiency by 50%. I realize that seems like an incredible number

(It sure does)

but I can back it up with research

(That's good my boss loves research)

I'd like to bring to you so you can judge for yourself.

Bill I've been with GIZMO for twenty years

(He's an old hand so he knows what he's talking about)

and I've never seen anything as good as this. I think you should take a look at it and I'd like to drop by and show it to you."

Now harken back to what is actually going through Smith's mind. We've established our credentials and warmed him up to our success in the past. This contact has job security written all over it. When the boss says:

"Why did you waste your time meeting with that clown from Gizmo"

Bill can say.

> "Boss, these folks from Gizmo may have something we need. They're a well-known company with ties to NASA. They have a partnership with IBM. They have lots of research data they want to show us. The guy who called is one of their senior management. If they're for real I think we need to see them."

Is this a career booster or what? Do the guys from Gizmo have credentials or not?

Even if this client's company is a small one, the very fact that Gizmo is connected with some of the largest companies in the world and is offering the same gee whiz system is an endorsement all by itself and automatically your product has instant credibility.

I realize that you may or may not have similar credentials as this imaginary wonder salesman from GIZMO but that's not the point. I exaggerated to help you see that you need to provide the prospect with comfort and a feeling of safety. His boss can hardly call him out for spending time to talk with such a well known firm and one with such credentials. Your firm may not have all those assets, but it has something that should give you and it credibility. Your credibility must be established with the very first contact.

It would be wise to realize that when a client agrees to meet with you they are putting their reputation on the line. That's why getting in the door is so difficult. They are taking a chance by bringing you in. If you end up being a waste of time they are going to have egg all over their face and that's not a good way to look good.

On the other hand they are also taking a chance by keeping you out. If your system is as good as you say and they didn't even take the time to see you, they are going to look awfully bad in front of the boss. They will balance those two choices and make a decision based on ... you guessed it ... the way they are going to look. In other words...what's good for them. The person who called the meeting is going to either look good or bad. They share in the glory or the gloom.

> *"Smith, why did you waste my time with that clown"*

or

> *"Smith, those guys from Gizmo might be just the ticket. That was real heads up way to handle this"*

But what about the situation where he doesn't commit to a meeting? How do you know where you stand?

Every sales call has two phases. The first phase (which is where we are right now) involves establishing our credibility and the parameters of the product.

Start Selling Smart!

Emotionally from the client's point of view they have to decide if you and your product are going to fit. If there is a need that you can fill, then you can move on to Phase two which is a determination of the suitability of the product. This is where all kinds of questions are going to be asked to determine the size of the waves your product is going to produce if it's taken aboard.

All products produce waves. The size of the wave is directly related to how upsetting the product will be to the current lily pond, which is our client's personal domain.

Before you called with your widget, the pond was quiet. The client had everything under control. No waves, only a minor ripple here and there. Now in you wade with your widget. Your widget has the potential to upset the entire pond. Production might have problems with it, Sales might be unhappy, the lawyers may pound on the desk and Management might run screaming from the building. (Hopefully none of those things will happen.)

HOWEVER your client doesn't know that yet. After he's mentally tried to imagine how you and your widget are going to fit into the pond, he can decide whether to take this to Phase two. That's when the serious fact checking, emotional temperature taking and negotiating takes place. If our guy is also able to commit to a sale there will be a shift from "*Hi howdy, how do you do,*" to " *what's the price, what's the delivery time, who's going to suffer the most (more on this last item later)?"*

That's how we can tell if we are going to get a meeting EVEN THOUGH HE HASN'T SAID A WORD about a meeting.

You can tell how you're doing by listening to the questions that are asked. As soon as your presentation moves beyond a very general description and a review of your credentials, we are into the meat and potatoes of the sales call. If he determines that you and the product are going to make too many waves, he won't waste his time determining how much, how many and how painful. He won't care. The conversation will pretty much end right there. He won't necessarily tell you that the party is over but you can bet that the funny hats and confetti are already on the floor.

Instead he will indicate that he has another meeting and *"..Give me a few days to think about this and I'll get back to you."*

That's when you analyze how far into your pitch you got. If the conversation never got beyond *'howdy do'* then it's not going to.

If he likes what you have and wants more information, then (as we said) you are into the meat and potatoes.

The more specific the questions the more interested he probably is. The longer the conversation, the closer you are to an actual sales meeting. Does that mean you have a sale? Hardly. It means that he is going to talk about it with others. How many others, we don't know. But if he's going to talk to others he needs more information than a '*howdy do*'. He needs to know how much, how many and how painful. He will ask a few of those questions so he can bounce them off others. That might be his boss, it might be one of the other departments. It depends on the product and the amount of disruption your product might cause.

Let's assume that Bill is willing to set up a meeting. Now, he'll set a meeting with you either with just himself or with some staff members. Here's where that VP's first name comes in. If Smith agrees to set up a meeting then casually ask,

"Will Alice be there?"

He'll either say "*yes*" or, "*no*" or, "*I don't know.*" And with those answers will come a mother lode of information that will be useful to you. Why? Ordinarily you would think "*Yes*" means she will be there. "*No*" means she won't. "*I don't know*," means maybe.

SO WHAT?

Let's take each possible answer and analyze it from the client's point of view (bearing in mind that the words

"*Yes*" "*No*" and "*I don't know*" in this situation carry a lot more meaning than in a casual conversation).

After all, the prospect has now committed to see you. He or she has already told you that they are intrigued enough to take time to listen to what you have to say. So Bill has to choose to see you alone or let his boss see it right away. AND THAT can tell you a lot about what the company is thinking. Why is that?

Remember we have already figured out the rough hierarchy of the company or at least of the Procurement Department. Smith reports to Simpson. So a "*Yes*" either means that she attends all meetings which means Smith has absolutely no power to say 'no 'and make it stick at all or he knows she will want to be in on THIS meeting.

If he is going to bring in the VP of Operations, his boss, without a prior meeting with you, it means that he thinks your widget has a lot of potential. And that is actually very revealing. Your pitch might be good but frankly, I doubt if it is that good. There is some reason that he thinks you are going to make him look good when you bring this in. Now why would that be?

Has someone in the company been talking about your Widget system?

Has Simpson said she was interested in making a change to their interoffice communications?

Has someone heard about GIZMO and the great work they do?

Right now we don't know exactly, but we do know that we have a LOT of interest for him to stick his neck out this far.

What about a "*No*"?

A "*No*" means that for some reason he isn't comfortable that he wants his boss to see this product yet. That could mean he is uncertain if you are legitimate or not, or if the product will do what you say, or if his company actually has a need for this particular product.

Now why would he take that position? Either he views his job as being the gatekeeper for all products that are to go up the chain of command or he has a special reason to want to vet this product and you before taking it further.

But what if he isn't sure if he wants his boss to attend or not? That's what *I DON'T KNOW* means . . . there is no clear cut policy regarding this kind of purchase and Bill is uncertain of where he is in the command structure. This probably means he is NOT the key person who can say "*yes*" and make it stick. An *I DON'T KNOW* means you must get through to the person who can say "*YES*" and make it stick and the only way to do that is to find out who attends the first meeting.

Now remember the little simple question we asked the SWITCHBOARD operator back on page 128? (*"May I have Ms. Simpson's first name please?"*) That little question set up our ability to ask Smith if his boss was going to be there, which in turn allowed us to get an answer from Smith (*Yes, No, I Don't Know*) which can give us a lot of information about

- How that meeting will go.
- Who might be the right person to make the buying decision.
- How open the company is to new ideas.
- How strong a position Smith is in.
- How much interest there is in the product.

The answer to this one simple question ("Alice") also has placed you on an entirely different level than as just the rep from GIZMO with a Widget to peddle. How can that be?

Now ordinarily you wouldn't even have asked *"May I have Ms. Simpson's first name please?"* So you wouldn't have been in a position to ask Bill if Alice would be at the meeting. By using her first name you are telling Bill something he might like to know. What is that?

Since you know his boss's first name you seem to know his boss. Not only that but you know his boss well enough to know her first name. YOU are on an entirely different level. He has got to think (My goodness, this guy knows Alice Simpson, MY BOSS.) Now he has to treat you and this meeting very seriously. Why?

Well, how would you feel if a voice on the phone asked about a good friend of his, YOUR BOSS? Wouldn't you instinctively regard that person as a powerful person, perhaps more powerful than yourself? I would. AND THAT GIVES YOU AN EDGE. It's not going to close the sale of course. The truth is you DON'T know Alice Simpson and she has never heard of you. Bill doesn't know that. If he goes to Alice and asks if she knows who ever it is from Gizmo. She will probably say :

"Well I don't remember the name but Gizmo I know."

SO WHAT?

So you are now able to go into that meeting with a lot more moxie than just as a peddler with a product. Let's face it, which would you rather be: someone from sales with a product to peddle OR a potential heavy weight from GIZMO with a possible wire into his boss and an IBM designed product backed up by research that will blow the doors off the ACME company?

It's always about them and their comfort level. In a fight who do you want backing you up a boy scout or the NYPD SWAT team?

SMART SELLING is giving you a heck of an edge. Don't believe me? Look at what would ordinarily have happened.

Ordinarily a salesperson would just pick up the phone and wrangle a meeting with somebody at ACME. There would be no questions asked at the switchboard or any selling going on until the meeting. It's just business as usual. Right?

Most salespeople will be driving to the ACME Company completely unaware that they are way behind the eight ball. Here they are whistling happily to themselves as the creep through the traffic and:

1. How do they know they're meeting with the right person? If they aren't meeting with the right person the product won't get a fair hearing. If they're lucky that person may take pity on them and give them the name of the right person. Is this where you want to be? NO.

2.The right person won't know who they are until they knock on their door. Is this good? NO.

3. Does our salesperson have any idea who they are meeting with beyond a title? NO.

4.Do they know where that person fits in the company structure? NO.

5.Have they prepared the ground for this first meeting by preconditioning the client with their overwhelming credibility and credentials? NO. They won't have done any of that. They're just a happy salesperson whistling to themselves as they creep along the highway and their client won't even remember that they are meeting with them today.

Compare that with the SMART SELLING approach. We now know a bit about:

1. Who is who i.e. who is running the department.

2. Who is in charge of procurement.

3. Who may or may not have the power to make a buying decision.

4. We established ourselves and our credibility.

5. We preconditioned the client into thinking positively about this meeting.

6. It's even possible that we impressed him enough that he is clearing his calendar and reserving a conference room and calling associates. In short he's taking this seriously and looking forward to our meeting today.

Is this better? You bet it's better. It's a smart way to sell!

CHAPTER NINE

READING THE COMPANY

SMART SELLING can be used with people because people have emotions and express those emotions in various ways, which can be revealing. But did you know that a company has an attitude, which it can express in similar language. And just like people the attitude of the company is revealing. How the company is laid out and what it considers important can give you a very valuable insight into how the company will treat you and your product. Here's an example of what I mean:

I was once about to hire a new San Francisco law firm to handle some very important litigation. The receptionist showed me into their beautiful glass enclosed conference room. The three lawyers I was considering joined me in the conference room.

"Nice conference room " I said.

"It is" One of them agreed. *"But wait till you see this"*

And he pushed a button and the curtains slowly were pulled back to reveal an absolutely stunning view of the Oakland Bay Bridge. He thought I was going to be impressed. But you know what I thought? I thought:

' This is where my money will be going. It has got to be really expensive to get a view like this. But I don't want to pay for a great view. The view actually is going to get in the way. I have serious business to discuss and if they think it's more important to have a great view then how serious can they be? If my business is going to be conducted in this room no one will pay much attention to what I need. They'll be staring out the window and at these prices I don't need to have them looking out the window.'

So I didn't hire that law firm based on something as petty as their magnificent view. What they thought was a deal closer was a deal killer. They had a different point of view than I did and I was the one who was going to have to pay for it. Except of course, I didn't hire them. Oh by the way, three years later that company closed it's doors. Maybe it was the high rent for that great view, who knows?

That's why the way a company looks can tell you a lot about what the company thinks. So you can apply SMART SELLING to reading the building and the layout too. It starts from the moment you pull into the parking lot.

Here we are at ACME INC. Let's say it's a typical building in a typical office park. What are the kinds of businesses that are in this particular office park? Is it an assortment of different types or are they more or less the same. If they are more or less the same, all in technology, or all in manufacturing for example there's a good chance they all signed there leases about the same time. Are they all start-ups or is there a well-known name among the tenants. A well-known name means the whole place might be pretty solid. A group of obscure start-ups means your client might be shaky.

We walk in the front door. What do we see? Businesses just like people have a body language all their own. It can be read just like a living thing. Companies have waiting rooms, conference rooms, offices etc. Each of these areas can tell you things about what the company values.

We probably will see a receptionist. We will see a reception room. We look about and see if there are other salespeople or clients or suppliers. We notice if the receptionist is ALSO the switchboard operator. All these things tell us a bit about how big and how busy ACME is.

We want to see a bustling and busy place. We want this company to need our system and if its dead quiet, our system is going to be a lot less appealing to them. If it's quiet, these folks don't need more efficiency, if it's dead, they need more business. So LOOK FOR ACTIVITY. You want a company that is busy. Phones should be ringing and people should be working and things should be happening. If they are not . . . be cautious. There is a reason. Perhaps this might be a company that is on the way out which means cutting costs AND IMPROVING EFFICIENCY would be a top priority. Look around and count the chairs in the reception area. That's right ...COUNT chairs.

If there are a few chairs in the reception area . . . obviously they don't expect very many visitors. If they have few chairs and the chairs look brand new NOBODY is calling on them. Is that because they are newly formed or snake bit?

CHECK THE MAGAZINES THAT ARE SCATTERED ABOUT The kinds of magazines tell you a lot about the company. If they are industry related then these folks are taking themselves very seriously. How do you know that? Generally the magazines are passed around from department to department. After everyone has read it, it ends up on the table out front for the visitors. If the magazines are general interest magazines, then no one in the company is that interested in what is going on in their field. These guys aren't very aggressive or competitive. They not interested in being on the cutting edge.

On the other hand if the magazines are closely tied to their business at least a few people are interested in the latest technology. Have you ever noticed the magazines in your dentist's office or your doctor's office? Almost all will have general interest magazines because they know there patients will be sitting and waiting for a while and they want to keep them from fretting. But some have magazines that deal with their specialty and handouts that deal with typical problems and drugs that are in their field. The salespeople who call on them provide these. That's important. If you're a drug salesman THESE ARE YOUR COMPETITORS. So pay attention. It tells you what the client is buying.

The same is true of any business. Look at the promotional materials, pens, calendars, clocks, coffee mugs etc. that have a logo on them. You'll see them on the receptionist's desk or somewhere around the lobby. Executives often give the receptionist stuff they don't want that a salesman has left. It's a dead give away for who has been here before. That's valuable intelligence for you ... if you pay attention to it.

If you study the magazines and brochures in the lobby it can give you a clue where the client's interest lies.

Are there lots of magazines about golf, or fishing or cars? Someone is interested in these. But who? Read the mailing label. If it coincides with the person you are calling on then you know what their personal interest is. This can give you some common ground. If you both like golf this can be a conversation starter.

Is this information going to close your sale? NOPE. But you never know when it is useful to know that the person who you are trying to sell ALSO happens to like golf as much as you do. All this information is just lying around for anybody to pick up.

Now answer truthfully. Haven't you been in a reception room just like this? What information did you process from what you saw? Did you learn who is who and what is what just from walking thru the front door.? If you paid attention to the little things, the magazines, the number of chairs, the condition of the rug, the hustle and bustle (or the lack of hustle and bustle) then you're using SMART SELLING

Now look at the clock. If the meeting is set for 10 you want to be there just a shade before 10 but not at 9:30. Try to be there right on the dot. 10 o'clock. Not sooner and not later. But why?

Doesn't the early bird get the worm? Remember that little innocent question we asked the switchboard operator a while back? *What is Ms. Simpson's first name?* That set up a cascade of information. If you are right on time not early (and certainly not late) you'll be able to use that punctuality to release a similar cascade of information and that will help you sell this guy. Here's how that works.

We want to use every scrap of information we can glean to make a sale. Being right on time . . . on the dot does several things that will make this sale easier...some obvious and some (of course) not so obvious.

Obviously, if you're right on time you are a person who can be relied upon to do things on time. It's good for your reputation. So it helps establish your credibility. That's obvious. But what is not obvious is that if you come exactly on time you can tell:

1.The kind of company you are dealing with . . . their corporate culture

2. Are they going to pay on time?

3. What they think of you and your company

4. How this sale is going to go. Will they be easy to deal with or not? Will you have to hold their hand and push to get this sold?

5. What to stress in your pitch?

How in the world can you tell all that from just showing up on time? Remember Sherlock Holmes?

It's the little unconscious things that reveal the truth. What kind of things can you find out by showing up right on the dot?

If they're ready for you exactly at 10, they have it together. This is a good sign because a business that runs on a clock is efficient. Punctual people pay bills on time. They will expect their employees to perform their tasks in a timely way. This means they won't waste their time or yours. That's why they are on time. See?

So, stress punctuality in your pitch.

If these guys have gotten it together and everything runs like clockwork, you want to be sure and stress in your presentation that your company runs like clockwork too. THEY WILL WANT TO KNOW THAT. They will be wondering about that. It gives you an opportunity to impress them with how organized and punctual your company is. With this expensive WIDGET system, reliability is going to be important and you have already started selling . . . just by showing up right on the dot.

But what if (Opps) . . . they make you wait. If you get there at 10 and they keep you waiting just a few minutes, it's not a disaster. It probably means that your contact is rounding everybody up and that's normal.

But if you are waiting for a long time, they are giving you valuable information. If they are really late:

1. You aren't considered very important or for some reason they want you to cool your heels. You and your product aren't being taken very seriously. If you and your company were considered important they would have someone waiting for you or at least they would send someone to explain what the delay was.

Start Selling Smart! 159

By the way, if they make you wait, don't feel badly.
It just means you have to impressive them some more. It means your credibility isn't completely established yet. So that tells you to build more credibility by stressing additional credibility facts about you and your company.

2. A long wait could mean they aren't very organized. If that's the corporate culture at this place you've got a lot of work ahead of you.

You are going to have to push them all through this sale. They won't be responsive. They won't return phone calls. You'll have to keep after them to keep things moving.

3. If your contact can't arrange a timely meeting he or she probably doesn't have a lot of clout. This will be confirmed when you see who is in the meeting.

All you did was show up and look what you can learn.

Now notice what would have happened had you gotten to ACME early (the early bird and that worm idea) and they KNEW you were early. First of all they would still keep you waiting because you would then have given them extra time to round up their people and reserve the room and appear punctual even if they actually aren't. You'd be acting as an alarm clock for the guy who is setting this up. So getting there early . . . the early bird, not only won't get the worm . . . you'd be letting the worm get away. Doing what you might think would impress them not only won't impress them, it will keep you from learning something they would never want you to know. Here's what you would have missed

1 How organized they are.
2 What their corporate culture is like.
3 What you should stress in your presentation to fit into their corporate culture.
4 Will they pay their bills on time?
5 Will you have to carry them through this deal?
6 Will they waste your time?
7 How powerful your contact is.
8 How you rank on their totem pole.
9 What additional credibility building you need to do.

Why would a sales person miss out on all this information? The answer is simply that they never realized that it was available for such a little amount of effort. Instead of paying attention to what the company is communicating in their treatment of a new visitor they are focused only on their presentation.

It is as important to observe the company in action, as it is to observe each individual in a meeting in action. Those actions give you information you can use. The average sales person doesn't realize that being early isn't a time saver it's an information waster. They are actually crippling themselves or at least making this sale much harder than it has to be. These self centered salesmen check in early and then have no idea how organized their prospect is and without that, they have no idea of what kind of corporate culture they face. They've missed out on a peek into the kind of clout their contact has. They won't be able to judge what the clients' present attitude is toward the product, their company or themselves. They will have no idea if this client is going to waste their time, need extra handholding or how seriously they are taking the whole process. They will miss this not because they were late but because they were EARLY!

While we are at it let's consider the kind of message you are sending if you show up late.

How much harm does it do? Please don't tell me:

"It's ok to be a little late, because after all I'm a busy guy"

IT'S NOT OK.

Being late to an appointment starts the client worrying about just how reliable you actually are. Since it is ALL about your credibility, you have just managed to start by putting a big hole right in the middle of your image. Can this be good?

Being late to anything or with anything is the worst thing you can do. It is absolutely intolerable. It says you are disorganized and that this sale means little to you.

Now that isn't you is it?

Yet the fact remains that a lot of salespeople don't connect how important being punctual is. You are not doing your client the favor of showing up! You are selling them something! If you are lackadaisical about that what does it say about your attitude toward the delivery of presentation materials or samples or (goodness gracious) MONEY?

Salespeople who are late, love to make excuses for themselves . . . *that's just me . . . I'm always five minutes behind. HA HA!.*

That five minutes can really cost you. I have met so many salespeople who are so disorganized it's amazing they get to work fully dressed each day. Some NEVER show up on time. Their clients soon take their lateness for granted.

> *"Oh JOE from BLANK CO. The guy is never on time. We don't have to worry about him. When he gets here we'll start to get our act together"*

Not a very good way to begin a presentation is it? So punctuality makes an impression. Yes, it's subtle. Yes, it won't close the sale. But as we have already said (and you are probably beginning to realize)

SMART SELLING

IT'S THE LITTLE THINGS

SMART SELLING is a series of subtle impressions that add up to a high level of comfort for the client that you can deliver and that your product and your company are the best.

OK now they're ready for you. Who actually comes out to greet you? Depending upon who that person is you would deduce

1. What kind of relationship the client wants.
2. How powerful your client is.
3. How secure he or she is in his or her position.
4. How impressed they are with your credentials.
5. How interested they are in your product.
6. How serious a prospect this actually is.s

Who is it? Is it your contact Bill Smith or someone else? If it's Bill Smith, he wants to greet you himself and this is a very good sign. He wants to get the cut of your cloth and set you at ease. He is telling you that he thinks you are on at least the same level as he is. He is really very interested. He will give you a fair hearing. It also means that your earlier conversation made him a little worried about how important you are. He doesn't want to take a chance and offend a friend of his boss. This position can be useful if things get tough in the meeting.

If he sends someone else, he wants to impress you. He is sending an emissary. He's trying to establish a position. It's a formal meeting. He's an important guy. This is serious.

This is fine. He IS an important guy (maybe). You want him to be serious. You're a serious person and this is serious business. You also know that he wants you to feel he's important (whether he is or not). He could just be trying to impress you. You must be admitted into his presence. That would mean that he feels vulnerable or at least has a pretty high opinion of himself.

If he sends someone else this is a pretty useful clue on how to treat the meeting. He represents your first contact and the way into the company. Don't get his feathers ruffled. This may not be the kind of person who will react well to a "*Howdy*" back slapping friendly sort of opening. You had better be a little more formal. This also means that you should let him control the first few moves of this meeting since he is making such a demonstration of authority.

As that person leads you from the reception area to your meeting room, pay attention to what is going on around you. Remember you are now walking through the company and the kind of company and it's attitude will be displayed all around you.

Are there a lot of empty desks (Perhaps some layoffs have recently occurred).

Is there a lot of buzz of busy people?

How many photocopiers or printers do they have?

How new is their equipment?

How are the employees dressed?

What's the feel of the company...are people tense or relaxed?

Observe the décor...is it cutting edge modern or more traditional? (This can give you a cue as to the type of presentation they will like)

Do they have conference rooms? (If so they have lots of group meetings. If not each department might be autonomous.)

How are the individual offices or cubicles decorated? (It says a lot about the employees' interests and sophistication. That gives you an insight into the type of person they hire.)

Is the carpet new or well worn? (Is there very little traffic or lots of back and forth bustle)

How do subordinates interact with their superiors? (If you've been met by the Sr. VP of sales and everyone calls him 'Joe', it tells you a lot about his management style.)

If Joe's secretary has come to get you then how do the employees treat them? If they're deferential, then Joe has some big time influence in the company.

How big is the company? Is it sprawled all over the place or is it small and compact? (This can tell you if you're in the home office of an outer satellite office. If you're out in the boonies and your product is pricy you have a longer road to travel)

Is there a company break room and if so are there vending machines and if so what are they vending? (Food products in the vending machines mean employees stay late and can't take time for lunch. Candy and soft drinks mean they rarely eat at their desks)

Is there a display of awards? (It can tell you a lot about morale and attitude. If they have a string of bowling or softball etc. trophies then the employees work together well and play together after work)

If you can get a glance at a bulletin board with messages for the staff it can tell you what they are concerned about.

Start Selling Smart! 167

Where is your client's office? (Corner offices really do carry weight in companies)

If you walk by the CEO's office and it's empty it could mean that he's out of town a lot and authority will be delegated.

All of this information is right there in front of your nose. Most salespeople wouldn't even notice it. They won't have a clue who they are dealing with, what the company values, how solid the company is, where their prospect ranks, what kind of presentation they will expect, how to handle the relationship.

But you will ...simply by paying attention.

CHAPTER TEN

ONE ON ONE

From your telephone conversation you have planted some valuable information that will serve you well in your upcoming face-to-face meeting. Hopefully you have already established that you represent a solid company with an expertise building your particular widget and that you have the skills to really be able to help him or her. So he or she will be primed to receive you in the best possible light. And all of this was done subtly with a minimum of talk and a lot of insight into the unconscious needs and behavior that drives any human interaction.

So let's assume that you are meeting with just one person, the keeper of the keys, the gatekeeper to this particular piggy bank. What you say and who you are talking to at this meeting is critical to your survival.

Let's say that he sent someone to bring you to him. So you know he wants a formal presentation.

Notice where he sits. If he sits behind his desk, he's leaving a barrier between you and him. That means he wants a formal presentation and needs a discrete space. Keep this in mind as you present. Does he stand up to shake your hand or remain behind the desk? Standing up is a sign of respect.

Does he offer you coffee or a drink? It means he wants to put you at ease. If he gets straight to the point you don't have much claim to his time and you better start with your credentials to slow him down. Otherwise you will be given the perfunctory five minutes and good by.

Does he tell his secretary to hold his calls? Or close his door? This indicates a sincere interest to concentrate on what you have to say.

Does he lean back in his chair as you begin (confidence and openness) or sit forward with his hands on the desk (business like and perfunctory).

Try to get him to reach over the desk by showing him a brochure or chart. However don't let him take or hold anything yet.

Why not?

You want him looking at you and listening to you not reading your presentation materials. You want to get and keep his attention. Why would you purposely distract him from you and your presentation by handing some knock out artwork designed to distract him?

If you hand out materials at the beginning of a meeting, then the client reads the materials rather than listening to you and you can't see their face and read their expression. So draw him to you but don't let him keep any of the materials.

As you work through your pitch look for expressions of surprise (Blink) satisfaction (Smile) dissatisfaction (frown or covering the mouth).

Notice the way he looks as he speaks to you. If he blinks and speaks, listen for something behind what he has just said. Does he ask rhetorical or obvious questions? Remember that generally means a hidden problem that you must resolve before leaving.

Does he look you directly in the eye (honesty) or away from you (deceptive)?

Does he glance at the phone (expecting a call or contemplating one . . . it could mean you're losing him)?

Look for combinations of words and gestures such as the ones we have already described to guide the way you answer his questions and subtly reinforce his comfort zone. Keep appealing to his self-image, job security and feeling of comfort.

Let him set the pace rather than going down your list of sales points. Pause frequently to smile and ask if he has any questions.

Give him the feeling that your company will back him up.

Most importantly RELAX. If you relax, so will he. The success of this call depends upon your feeling of confidence and belief in the product. If he believes you believe in what you are saying, he will be inclined to take your product seriously.

Often traditional salespeople will begin by talking of all sorts of things rather than getting to the point and begin the pitch. They want to "size up" the prospect.

It sounds impressive but you know what? It's baloney. They need time to decide what to say because they haven't done any pre-selling and now they have to make up for all that lost time. Fat chance! This sure is a fine time to finally start your sales pitch.

This, of course, will never happen to you since you will already have done all the preliminary work in advance by all the SMART SELLING you did as you set up this meeting.

So instead of floundering around for the first five minutes you can say a few off the topic sentences and smoothly begin. In the case where the client wants a formal presentation, take it seriously right from the beginning and begin. This doesn't mean you should be cold or dry. Be relaxed, open and informative.

Let's say you've finished your pitch. Your client sat through without fidgeting or playing with his pencil or glancing at his watch. He got it. Now what happens next is critical.

At the end of your presentation, he or she will lean back in their chair and say something. He may have asked you lots of questions and you will have given sparkling and comprehensive answers. Now it's time for the meeting to come to a close.

This leaves us with one of two possible outcomes. Either he has the power to say YES and make it stick or he doesn't.

If he has the power to make the call you are at the end of your quest. He either will go for it or not and you will know very quickly. He has no one to ask, no permission to get. It's quick. However he may have the power and still want permission from his staff. At which point he will want a further meeting. If he asks for some time to bring in people…STOP THE PRESSES. Cancel everything. Put off all other meetings until this baby is in the can. You are so close to a sale you should be able to smell it. LET HIM. HELP HIM. MAKE THE CALL FOR HIM (if you can).

Getting staff in to approve a potential product is as close to sales heaven as you are going to get. It won't necessarily be easy. But at least you have a good chance because YOU ARE THERE! You have all the answers (you should have all the answers, you know). So take that meeting immediately!

But it often isn't that easy, is it? Let's say...he does NOT have the power to make a final decision. This is the most likely scenario. He will need to consult with some one who does. If he is planning on making a presentation without you, he will ask you for a proposal, the artwork, a brochure, your presentation or something, which contains all the pertinent facts.

The reason he will give you is quite different from the real reason. He will say that he wants to study your proposal. This is true, but it also could mean that his mind is made up to kill this idea.

He will make it easy on himself by closing this meeting and waiting a day or two and then calling with a turn down. It is much easier than telling you right now that the company doesn't want this. That's the second day phone call scenario.

How do we know that he might kill your product?

SMART SELLING

THEY ALWAYS TRY TO KILL IT

Sorry it's just the way it is. The first impulse of every customer is to try to get this nuisance off their desk. Every product, every presentation is a potential job loser. Every phone call asking to present is risky to their long-term job security. It has nothing to do with you or your product. It's the nature of corporations that your ego rides on every decision. You don't build a career on committee attendance. (I understand this is different in Japan so if you are reading this in Japan, I apologize...it's different other places).

So any client must take a negative and hostile attitude at first. It's your job to protect your sale and convert them to a positive point of view. It's their job to try to pick holes in it and get it killed.

If you have a great product and great presentation and if you've been paying attention you can swing them from the enemy camp to one of your defenders. That's the goal. Once you have them on your side you can leave the room. Someone else will fight for you without trying to stab you in the back. But since this is just round 1...expect the worst. They WILL try to kill it.

This is generally done in the following way... he will want a presentation but not want you to present.. Why? He wants a weak representation of you i.e. your write up. Your write up might be good but it can't answer questions that the boss will ask. Only your client can. It's not fair perhaps but who said this had to be fair?

The real reason he is asking for these materials is to take them to his superior, the person who can make the final decision and he needs something to justify the spin he is going to put on this which will allow him permission to kill the deal or not. If he "studies" the materials you can't claim that he didn't evaluate the work thoroughly. Then he can do his job and present a biased accounting of the situation, which will get the project killed or if he isn't sure he wants it dead this will allow his boss to make the commitment and ask to hear more. This way he can't lose. If his boss agrees with the negative pitch he gives, too bad.. it gets turned down and you are gone. If his boss like what he hears, the boss will authorize him to spend more time on it and they will ask you back. It's very simple. It's cold blooded perhaps, but simple.

To avoid that we must try to get several people involved. Just like any murder, it's tougher with witnesses and that will mean, you must get past this meeting and on to another meeting, a meeting with you present.

If another meeting is set up, you can bet it means there will be several killers in the room with you who's sole purpose is to kill this product but that's OK. This is the most frequent scenario. The good news is that you will be there to defend the product and your company so that's the important meeting where all the forces will be fairly balanced.

Fair...Little you against all of them.

So how do you force the next meeting?

SMART SELLING

GIVE THEM A REASON TO CONSIDER THIS MORE

Remember the SMART SELLING rule that said you must give them a good reason to buy? Well...now you must also give them a good reason to consider your product in a larger meeting. With more people around you will get a thorough airing of all points of view and stand a chance. But it isn't as easy as shaking apples out of an apple tree. You've got to climb up the tree a bit to get at the apples and to do that you have to go out onto a limb a bit.

The way you go out onto a limb is by making a BIG PROMISE.

"We're so certain our widget system will perform the way we have said that we'll let you try it for FREE for two months."

or

"Bill, let me bring my people in here to give you an idea if it would be worthwhile to go with our system. If it isn't going to make 100% sense then we'll tell you and we'll drop the entire thing. What do you have to lose?"

This big promise deals with a gatekeeper's worst problem. He doesn't want to stick his neck out and wants you to instead. This way he can say to his boss:

> *"Boss, they volunteered to undertake a complete system check and give us their results. It won't cost us a penny. We might learn a lot on their nickel."*

Something free will satisfy his boss because it won't waste anyone's time. They can continue as they were, unruffled and let GIZMO waste their time. Of course if the analysis can't be done without disrupting their present operation that might present a serious problem. But as long as it won't cost ACME anything in time, or money, chances are they will go for it. You and your company are out on the limb. That's the risk you have to take but it guarantees you another meeting, with your staff as backup.

Ahh! But what about a third case? What if Bill has the power to make the decision and still asks for your material for further consideration. What does that mean?

Obviously even though he could turn you down flat right now you have made enough of an impression that he wants to at least appear to consider it. This means there is something that he likes. It could be you, it could be your company or it could be the product. Whatever it is asking to keep materials of any sort is a signal that there is merit in what you have said. It's an ember you can blow on to keep this deal hot and alive. How do you know? He will tell you if you are watchful and listen close. Depending on how he closes the meeting he will say something that will indicate what he's thinking.

And why would he do that?

He can't end a meeting without saying something about the meeting. Otherwise he would have been wasting his time and in business that's never allowed. So even if what he says is negative at least he will have spent his time in a reasonable way. SO SOMETHING has to come out of the meeting. Why tell you? He doesn't want to but he has to. It's an instinct.

We demonstrate to ourselves that we are accomplishing something by evidence. In this case he needs evidence that you were there and that a meeting was held. He needs something concrete. Even if he has made up his mind and isn't interested in the product, when he asks for materials, he wants to keep a token of it. This is a bit like tourists picking up post cards of place they visit. They want a memory. Your artwork or presentation or whatever is a post card remembrance. Having this souvenir says:

"See the bozo from GIZMO was here and now he's gone. Here's the remnant of his visit"

You can use that instinct to demonstrate a useful use of time to see into their mind. They always will signal something about the meeting at the end of the meeting. Remember the SMART SELLING rule...

THEY ALWAYS TELL YOU THE TRUTH AT THE END

Watch for it. Here are some other possible signals they might give:

> "Thanks for coming over. I'll review this and get back to you. YOU have a really interesting idea here."

He likes you and is giving you credit for the idea (even though it was your company that developed the idea).

> "Thanks for coming over. I'll review this and get back to you. GIZMO has a fine reputation for quality products."

Now why would he mention something about GIZMO? He is signaling that he is impressed with the company and wants to do business with them. But what if then he says:

> "The only thing that still bothers me is the cost of this. It's much more than we have budgeted."

Now you know that you missed setting this item to rest. But it's not too late. Here's your opportunity to say:

> "Bill, don't let the price thing worry you. We're a big company and can work out terms that will make it workable for you."

Or

> "Bill, be sure and review page 45 which shows you the analysis of savings that we've verified. Your company should easily do as well as that. If you want me to have our people do a preliminary review of your operation to confirm that.

Earlier we mentioned that you cannot leave any loose ends lying around to trip this deal up. So listen for any hint of a loose thread and nip it quick.

OK...you got to the next meeting. This is the biggie. Now what?

CHAPTER ELEVEN

SMART SELLING A ROOM FULL OF PEOPLE

Let's say that your contact liked what you had to say and has called a meeting of various folks from different parts of the company. He needs their input. This is a meeting that must be held with any company wide product. Each department has their own troubles and insights and this product has to satisfy every one of them. So each of these departments will be motivated to do the same thing that motivated Bill. They want to get on with their duties and not waste their time on your product. It's your job to take on their individual problems and dispatch them. The more efficiently you do that the easier it will be to gain allies.

A room full of different departments is like a see saw with you on one end and all of them on the other. You start off all alone way up there and little by little they will slide over to your side so that at some point you will have enough on your side to gain the upper hand.

Earlier we said that each person would have input in any meeting. They cannot remain silent. Even if they have very little to say, they must say something. However we also said that each of them would have their own pet peeve in their briefcase that you must handle. Here's what you should do to sell these folks:

Each person in the room is there for a reason. But what is it? They all were invited because they bring their own special expertise. Also it's impossible to bring anything into a company without everyone signing off on it. Since it's always about them they have to have a chance to look at it, sniff it, and decide if they approve. So now instead of 1 person to sell you have many. Each has his or her agenda. You have to consider ever ego involved and everyone's reputation is on the line. You cannot afford to alienate anyone. So . . .

SMART SELLING

THROW EVERYONE A BONE.

This means you must prepare something for each possible attendee at that meeting. You need something for Sales, and something for Marketing, and something for Production and so on. That "something" is a question, which they can answer in a positive way or a product benefit that they can consider and respond to in a positive way. Whatever it is, you must provide them a way to look good while approving this sale.

There are very severe penalties for not letting everyone have a bone. If you don't, you will be the bone the neglected party chews on. I'm perfectly serious about this.

The last thing you want is someone from Legal with no bone of a legal nature to throw at him. Careful ...he will find something to occupy his mind. He has to. How long do you think he would remain employed if at every meeting he attended, there were nothing for him to contribute? The boss, or at least the most senior person there, would start wondering:

"You know, I've seen Floyd in every one of these meetings, and he never has anything to say. Does he really have that much free time?"

Poor Floyd! He might have reams and reams of paperwork on his desk. He might be a brilliant legal mind and critical to the company's success. But he is on display right now. In this meeting, at this time, he is on display, just like you. He has to find a reason to look like he is important to this meeting, and he will find a reason.

What's a brilliant legal mind going to do? There has to be a reason he is attending this particular meeting. If you don't throw him a legal bone, he will focus in on every little nook and cranny of your wonderful widget until he finds something, even something inconsequential for that brilliant legal mind to zero in on. This you do not want!

I guarantee he will find something.

Remember:

SMART SELLING

EVERYONE IS ON DISPLAY AT A MEETING

NOT JUST YOU.

It is your job to make sure they all look good! Yes, I know you have plenty on your plate just selling your widget, and that this extra babysitting is not very appealing to you. But remember, this meeting is a sudden-death playoff game. If you are going to win it and move on to more games, you must play by the rules. The rules say that all the people in this room have to like your widget and like you. If you make each and every person feel important and useful, they will like you and go easy on your widget.

The good news is: This isn't that difficult. Well before your presentation, you are going to have thought about most of the problems that every department would probably have, so you should have plenty of bones to throw. With any bone that you throw be sure and know the answer and never ask for an opinion. Here's why:

Any successful trial lawyer will tell you that you don't want to ask your witness a question that might blow up in your face. You want to ask questions that you can control. Don't ask for opinions unless you know what the answer is going to be.

There is something else to keep in mind. It's a tactic to employ in your presentation, and it will both help you determine the pecking order in the meeting, and ease your way psychologically in among the ranks so that your client's people will begin to think of you, subconsciously, as one of them, instead of as an outsider presenting to them. It has to do with the seating arrangement in the room.

Here you are at ACME Corp with a room full of people. There will be a conference table that everyone will sit around.

Begin by noticing where they sit and who they sit with. Our feelings about people are expressed in how we arrange ourselves. People who are superior in power deserve respect from all the others. It's an instinct. Those in an inferior position will sit below them in order or give them lots of space around them. They are trying to show respect. This natural instinct goes way back to the way the elder in a tribe is treated. If you pay attention you can find out who the power players are and how powerful they are, just by observing the way others in the room treat them. Here's what I mean,

SMART SELLING

PEOPLE GROUP BY RANK OR INTEREST

In a large meeting, salespeople will ordinarily sit with Sales people, Production people with Production people, and so on. Why...because they know each other. They work together every day. Don't you sit with your friends when you go to the movies? Human beings of the same rank stick together.

If one member of Sales sits right next to someone from Brand...that tells you something. They have a close relationship and are accustomed to working together. If someone is new, he or she will appear unsure and won't know where to sit. This is revealing, because this person probably won't have much to say about your product, either.

Most important of all in discerning roles from seating choices:

SMART SELLING

PEOPLE WHO ARE VERY IMPORTANT

SIT IN ORDER OF RANK

The Senior Marketing Manager will sit next to his immediate subordinate, probably the Brand Manager or the Product Director. This is a courtesy that is completely unconscious. Everyone in that room is used to taking orders from the most senior person, and then the most senior person after that, and so on. That pecking order will even be followed in the way they sit. Often, the most senior person will sit at the head of the table with subordinates on either side. I call this position "The Power Spot."

Why do people do that? I think it's because that's the way we sat around the dinner table with Dad at the head of the table and Mom at the foot.

You will be the underdog at this presentation. There will be far more of them than there are of you. They will try to sit together on one side of the table. They will assume you are going to sit on the other side, so that it's their side against your side. I try to dispel the idea that we are in opposition by purposely moving to the same side of the table. I'm "on their side" that way. We are all symbolically on the same side. This forces them to spread out and breaks up pairs and triplets from the same department, and that's important.

Why is this important? Pairs and triplets from the same department can double and triple team you. That happens when two or three gang up on you with one asking one question and the other another question. I've been double-teamed like this, and it's not fun. They fire question after question at you just as if you were undergoing an assault. While one is asking, the other is thinking up something new to ask you. Your pitch ceases being a presentation and becomes an interrogation. The only thing missing is the rubber truncheon. This is very destructive to your case and to your control of the meeting. But if you can separate them, they will not feel that mutual support. They will be equal to you, and it becomes one on one again.

Now, obviously, if this is going to make it difficult for you to present, then it can't be done. But remember: You will probably be the first person in the room, or at least one of the first. So you will have the opportunity to sit where you can be most effective. Others will straggle in after they finish that phone call or cup of coffee or lengthy email. So they will scatter around the table. This has the effect of separating pairs and triplets from the same department. Instead here's what you should aim for:

SMART SELLING

ALWAYS TRY TO SIT NEXT TO

THE MOST IMPORTANT PERSON IN THE ROOM.

Notice I didn't say "across from." Why? Once again, you don't want the room to become them-against-you. You want to send the subconscious message that we are all on the same side. Power radiates from position. The most important person will probably be at the head or foot or the center. Your position next to him or her will mean that all the rest of his or her subordinates will think of you as nearly the boss's equal, so they will listen more attentively to what you have to say

Look, every little edge helps in these matters; so don't give an inch if you don't have to. There are so many subtle psychological currents running through a meeting that your seating position isn't 100 percent critical. Where you sit will not absolutely sink your presentation . . . but sitting in a power spot could help.

You will notice during the meeting that it is generally the senior people who will do most of the talking. What you must remember to do is always direct your answer to the most senior person, even if he or she hasn't asked the question. You do that by referring to "your company" and by making eye contact with the most senior person:

"Now you can see why we feel your company can increase efficiency by 50%."

We know that the decision maker is the only person who will make that final decision. So you must determine if he or she is present. In a large meeting you can locate them by observing the person or person(s) who called the meeting. They will either mention the decision maker or look right at him or her. If it's a one on one meeting assume YOU ARE LOOKING AT HIM OR HER.

The decision maker will sit in a power position either at the end of the table or in the middle. The various departments will arrange themselves by rank of importance and familiarity by sitting next to each other.

Obviously, you are here because there is sincere interest in your product and you have paved the way by establishing your company's credibility. You want to establish a relationship with everyone in the room. They will be introduced to you by the most powerful person in the room or by the person who called the meeting.

SMART SELLING

REMEMBER EVERYONES' NAME AND POSITION

To do that...write it down as quickly as you can. This is often very difficult to do since generally people want to get through meetings as quickly as possible. The best way is to just ask . . .

"Say wait a minute I want to keep everyone's position and name straight so let me jot it down."

Then do.

As an alternate hand out your business card and expect one from them. If they have NO business card they probably are new or don't count much. If they give you a business card LAY IT DOWN IN FRONT OF YOU AROUND A SQUARE THAT REPRESENTS THE TABLE. Use the business card like a place card at a dinner party

Start Selling Smart! 193

and mark everyone's' position in front of you in the same place as they are sitting. This way you can glance at the left side and know who is sitting where. If not everyone gave you a card, write down their name.

To read the room you have to know not only what the title is but also what the title means. Unfortunately an imposing title doesn't necessarily mean that the job is a big one or that the person has much weight. The best way to know is once again to ask. *"What is a vice president of corporate development actually?"* Is it Sales? Is it Marketing? Is it PR? ASK.

Incredibly most salespeople haven't a clue who is at the meeting even when given a business card. They don't care. And they don't ask. BUT YOU MUST. It's the interplay between these various departments, which will reveal where the power in the company is. The power I'm referring to is not power to chart the destiny of the company. The power you care about is the power to sign the contract.

The fundamentals of meeting behavior say that the person who called the meeting will introduce the most important people first and give a general overview of why the meeting was called. They may begin with excuses for various departments . . ."*Jim has an 11 o'clock and Sue needs to leave before 12 etc."* These parameters tell you your limits. If Jim is the director of Sales get to the end of your pitch before 11. If Sue is the

decision maker make sure you wind up well before.
These little excuses are really helpful since only important people need to give reasons to leave a meeting where their input is important. So when the excuses are made PAY ATTENTION.

You are aware that everyone at the table will want input and will need a bone to chew on so they can impress everyone else. This means your presentation takes a back seat to this all-important display. Let them use your product as a means for asking pertinent, sharp, probing and incisive questions. This makes them look pertinent, sharp, probing and incisive. To do that, ask each of them a question relating your product to their area of expertise. This allows them to probe for weakness (of which, of course, you have none).

Notice which member does the talking. It is generally a safe rule to assume that only the senior people will speak or ask questions. They are the most important. This is where you take out those SMART SELLING ears and listen. This is the place where your answers are used to push your agenda forward ever so slightly each time.

After you have run through most of your sales points and everyone has an idea of what your product can do for them. you must start to manipulate the room into agreement. You do this by leading each department into agreement with each other. This requires sensitivity and tact.

Since you know who is sitting where and have an idea of their importance. You then use their first name and ask questions that are designed to be answered in a positive way. This forces them to appear to agree (even if they don't).

As an example:

"Sid, every time I have presented this, Sales asks me about cannibalization of current product. It seems to me that this actually is a different market than you are currently reaching. At least that's what the folks at GE thought. But what's your thought?"

This allows Sid from Sales to pontificate on the terrible time his sales people have had selling the last product that was like this but that they succeeded after much labor and effort. Therefore he will agree with General Electric that the product isn't going to be cannibalistic. Yes, he's beating his chest and pointing out how hard he works and how good his guys are. That's fine. That's what has GOT to happen. We expect that. But by getting him to agree it's the OTHER departments who are now thinking that perhaps Sid is inclined to support this product. If Sid is a real mover and shaker he will influence everyone else. And you get the benefit from that assumption.

Notice that everyone will be making assumptions about who is going to support the product and who is not. If you have read the room correctly, you will be able to locate where the disagreement is coming from . . . Sales, Marketing, Legal, etc. That allows you to follow up with the troublesome department. Draw them out to find out where the problems are. There's always a reason they are reluctant to support you, especially if others seem to like it. So you need to focus their attention on the dissenting department.

What you are actually doing is using the peer pressure of the other departments of the company to get them to go along. Whatever the reason for their reluctance, it is important that you do not confront that reluctance directly. In other words don't say:

"Gee Joe what's the problem?" You will get a very angry response. If you have supporters then they will start to carry your water. Remember that by this time everyone knows what you and your product can do. The issue is not what can it do but shouldn't they buy it. The whole point of this meeting is to determine the feasibility of moving forward with this. AND WHO'S GOING TO DO IT?

Most of the time...WHO'S GOING TO DO IT? is the single most critical problem. Who's going to pay for it out of their budget? Who's going to provide the internal manpower for your product?

This makes perfect sense because:

SMART SELLING

YOUR PRODUCT IS NOT BEING BOUGHT

IT'S BEING ABSORBED

You and your company and your product must fit within their system. AND you have to make it very clear that you will melt into their system like butter on flapjacks. The lower your PAIN profile the better.

Remember earlier I mentioned that they were going to meet to determine who is going to suffer the pain? Inserting anything new into a corporate body is going to be painful. Routines have to be changed. Manpower needs to be trained. Computers have to be programmed. Etc. Etc. You have to convince them that this is going to be easy. HOW?

SMART SELLING

IF POSSIBLE VOLUNTEER TO DO IT.

The difficult part about selling anything isn't selling the product . . . it's doing the work your client is suppose to do. If you've done your selling right, you've sold your company's capacity to carry this off. They aren't buying your product; they are buying you and your company. If you want to get this job done in a reasonable time period YOU MUST DO MOST OF THE WORK.

This is where reading the room can be helpful. As you step forward to do most of the work, see who wants to get a piece of it and who does not. Depending upon the product and the potential for career development and success, you will find that some players are more eager to take the work on than others. They will show this in several ways.

They will volunteer to handle certain aspects. They will mention specific expertise or staff that should get involved. They will be enthusiastic. This CAN be very good if they are competent, supportive and have nothing to gain.

But as you might imagine, the kiss of death is to leave something important in the hands of an overeager climber, who is going to get in way over their head. Management will be inclined to let the climber learn on your nickel, so you must be careful when letting any part of your project out of your hands. A good rule of thumb is:

SMART SELLING

THE MORE YOU DO THE MORE GETS DONE.

You will know what your own company policy is regarding client involvement. Ordinarily if you own it and are installing it, get them to keep their cotton pickin' hands off of it. Nicely, of course.

Start Selling Smart! 199

Now that you have a pretty good idea of how the room is arranged, who the players are, where they are seated, who is in support and who has a hidden agenda, you can take out the SMART SELLING ears we discussed earlier and listen for each departments UNSAID concerns.

The easiest way to learn what questions is actually code for a problem is to have lots of selling experience. If you have been around the block a few times, you KNOW that the same problems occur in every company. For those of you who aren't quite so well experienced below is a list of questions from various departments that in one form or another indicate a problem that you must address.

SALES

Sales will worry about anything that takes up the salesman's' time. Their job is to make calls not sit in a meeting. So anything that is going to eat up time . . . training, sales meetings, contests, new products, changed products, new types of reports are all potential problems.

Generally these will be put forward as abstract concerns.

"Do you handle the training?" "How similar is this to (product X)." "How long does it take to get the staff up to speed?"

To all these questions the answer is not to assure them that it's a snap, a piece of cake, simple, easy and fun. It's not. They know it's not and you will blow a hole in your own foot if you try to walk down that road. Remember they are looking to you to do the work. You and your company must volunteer to handle all the training and remedial education that your product will require. If you can provide manuals, instructors, incentives, seminars all the better just as long as your customer doesn't have to do anything but show up.

MARKETING

Marketing will worry about allocation of resources. Media support, collateral materials, handouts, brochures, etc. Once again you are going to have to provide all this support. But the biggest problem you are going to face isn't the Marketing department; it's the company's advertising agency. THIS CAN BE A BIG PROBLEM and it won't be mentioned in the clear. The agency will fight like demons to keep your cotton pickin fingers off the media budget. They won't take kindly to any funding you might take that they could use. You are going to have to make it appear that they are involved and taking the lead even when the truth is they don't know which direction to march. You'll pick up on this when the VP of Marketing says something like:

"Are you familiar with Shoefly, Pander and Yawn our agency?" "How do you work with outside ad agencies?."

Or worst of all . . . *YOU are going to LOVE working with Shoefly. They are terrific.* "

What the VP of Marketing is actually anticipating with this statement is World War 3. Why? The agency is going to try to kill this deal and they will use every trick in the book to blow it up. Taking this product on means nothing but grief for them. They make their dough out of the media buy and diverting media funds to support this new product isn't going to sit well. The VP of Marketing doesn't want to tell them. He wants you to take on the job of telling them that their anticipated budget for this year has just gone up in smoke. It means less money for them and more for you. This will cause an explosion. He wants to be out of town when this happens in case they get really mad because then he's going to have a terrible time keeping them happy with next years budget.

However if YOU take the heat he can profess ignorance of the damage and blame it on *"a new corporate direction."* After all they can't blame him if the crystal ball gazers at the top have changed course right in the middle of what should have been a carefully laid out marketing plan. So as far as Marketing will be concerned they are just following orders. As long as he can get you to take the gas pipe, he's off the hook. If you won't do that then they will drag their feet. So you have a choice here. Either you do it and the project moves forward or you don't and the Marketing department drags its feet all the way through this.

PRODUCTION

Production will always watch the clock. They have to turn out product. They have to do it on a timetable. They have to have parts, components, raw materials and whatever else your product requires. They want it flowing freely and in abundance. They want you in the coal bin shoveling like crazy to keep the furnaces stoked.

Remember the guy in production who wondered about the availability of parts?

That's the kind of question you can expect. Questions with the keyword . . . AVAILABILITY, TIMELYNESS, COMPLEXITY, and ASSEMBLY. Those words all mean the same thing and require pretty much the same answer.

"YES we are prepared to cover you to the eyebrows with whatever you need, we will move heaven and earth to make sure you get them before you even know you need it."

LEGAL

Legal worries about liability. To them behind every sale is a potential lawsuit. They are currently overwhelmed with work, so you and your product are one more log on the already too highly piled log pile. They are going to want assurance that your legal department will do everything and keep them out of it. To do that they will probe around liability issues, past law suits, potential sour customers. "Have you considered this ?" kind of questions. Your answer is that you are prepared to take it all on and do it, that you have patents, copyrights, hold harmless agreements and the last will and testament of every single one of their potential customers. If anyone makes a peep, your legal team must be all over them like warts on a bullfrog. They want your promise of constant quiet and tranquility all at your expense of course.

MANAGEMENT Management is looking for only one thing from you. . . . COMMITMENT. They want you and your company to walk the plank for even the smallest infringement. They want you to be there at every moment from the time they sign the contract until the stars go out all over the sky. They want you to walk this all the way through and they don't want to be bothered with any decisions. Any time someone in any of the other departments has a problem YOU are expected to solve it. They expect they will never see you or your product again except as a profitable entry on the balance sheet.

Now none of this will be spoken out loud of course. But the message will be sent and guess what? Whatever it is that they want THAT'S WHAT YOU ARE GOING TO GIVE THEM.

SMART SELLING

GIVE THEM WHAT THEY WANT

Isn't this somewhat unreasonable? Perhaps but remember you are the one who came to them with all these promises nicely listed in your sales brochure. You must keep those promises and then go way beyond that if you expect to remain one of the boys. Actually that's the price of selling the product. As we mentioned earlier it has little to do with the product, it comes down to you and your company and what you can do for them. No matter what you do for them, it won't be enough. But then they have the checkbook and you don't.

The rewards for this overabundance of service will be very substantial. As "one of the boys" you will be asked to attend meetings and be given the opportunity to offer them additional products and services.

THIS IS A BIG DEAL.

Instead of making 10 sales of a single product after 10 sales calls; you will make 10 sales of 10 different products with 1 sales call. So your reward will ultimately be SUPEREFFICIANCY. So it is definitely worth it. You won't get there if you aren't at their elbow constantly. When they turn around . . . you will be there with a helpful suggestion and a suitable recommendation. This is where SMART SELLING can get you.

Contrast that with where most salespeople would be. They might have a single sale. Every department in the client's company will be ignorant of their company's products and potential. They will be anonymous. When a problem comes up, the client won't even remember their name, let alone know what number to call. So this means that each and every time they have to start all the way back at ground zero with a cold call. It's like climbing the same mountain all over again. All the same risk and effort with no better prospect for success. THIS IS NOT SMART. This is making the entire process much harder than it has to be.

So if all this service and attention seems like a lot of effort remember that if you put the effort in now you will be able to make future sales with much less effort.

SMART SELLING

WHAT YOU PUT IN NOW WON'T BE REQUIRED LATER

Exactly how your sales pitch will go depends upon your product and your personal approach. With SMART SELLING however you will know who is who and what is what and be prepared to answer the unasked.

CHAPTER TWELVE

WHAT SMART SELLING CAN DO FOR YOU

We've seen how SMART SELLING can really take a lot of the heat out of a presentation. By understanding what is bothering the client, we can be sure to answer all those unasked questions, which might be too sensitive for them to actually ask. By releasing all those unspoken but worrisome bonds tying the boat to the dock, you free the client to follow their desire. Instead of pounding away with sales point after sales point, we found that all we had to do was slip the rope that was holding the client back. It just requires a little insight and a little interest.

We've seen how SMART SELLING will give you an extra edge. I'm sure you've seen sales people who always know the right thing to say. They always seem to know what to do in any situation. And they seem to do it instinctively without hesitation and with little prompting. Perhaps you felt they were just a "natural." There are indeed such people. But unfortunately not all of us are so lucky. To the vast majority of us therefore SMART SELLING gives you a guide, a road map toward the sale. It will help you listen to your customer and see things through their eyes. That is turn will keep you concerned, and involved with their company. We've seen how to hear not only what the client is saying, but what they are not saying. It might not be mind reading but it comes pretty close. Your customer will appreciate your insight and understanding. There's no better way that I know to build a long lasting partnership. Such relationships lead to more repeat sales and better profits for everyone involved. .

Each of us approaches the sale in a different way. SMART SELLING can give you an approach that at the least can help you see things from the point of view of the client and at the best, help you change from a peddler into a consultant. The overall goal is to improve the way the company sees you and your product. These tools and this approach hopefully will open the door into their company. They will take you in. They will make you one of the boys. You will be a trusted partner in their business.

We discussed how sensitivity to their unspoken concerns could lead them to depend upon you. IF you make them lean on you for their job security, you will be holding a very powerful position. It will pay big dividends since you will not only get repeat after repeat sale, but over time expand the number of items you are selling to them. IN some cases they might actually call you just to ask for advice!

These tools can give you insight into what is going on when a client asks questions that on the surface seem rather simple or even downright silly. You now know how to respond to questions that are actually requests for information rather than confrontation. With this approach unlike your standard sales approach, the client will be setting the pace and absorbing the information at their pace not at yours. This will allow them to take you into their business and build your product into their system.

You will find that SMART SELLING helps you gauge the client and the speed of your presentation. By linking your remarks to the rate at which your client absorbs what you are presenting, you will find that they set the pace. This will keep you from either overwhelming them with too much information or moving along too slowly. The client will unconsciously feel in control and that will make your sale simpler. You won't be fighting their feeling of not being in control. After all, it's their money and they aren't going to be pressured into let go of it. It's your job to help them accept the product because they see that it will fit and not feel that they were forced. That's the perfect combination for a sale that remains sold. You don't want the wheels to come off down the road because buyer's remorse sets in and they feel you rammed the product down their throat. If they set the pace, you'll raise their comfort level. The higher the level is, the easier the sale is going to be.

So I suppose you are wondering how quickly you will be able to use all this new information?

Start now. At first just listen to what your clients are saying. Then later when you start noticing those rhetorical questions and loaded inquiries start linking what they are doing to what they just said. It's a balancing act. Over time you'll find that you naturally start hearing alarm bells and changing your presentation in response. You don't have to do it all in one meeting. But little by little drag this book out and skim over some of the chapters to refresh your mind on what to think about when you see and hear your client doing something that is a little out of the ordinary.

Shortly much of this will become second nature. You won't even think about it. You'll see or hear something and automatically change course in your presentation to match the direction the client is moving.

Probably the first thing you'll find is that you start closing sales you never thought you'd get and that your relationship with your clients starts changing from a sales person to client relationship to one of advisor to client. It will be much more personal and much more rewarding (not to mention more profitable).

If just some of these things happen, you will have made your sales job much easier. And that has been our goal all along. By Selling Smart you will improve your efficiency, make more and not have to work so hard to get where you want to go.

I'd like to hear how you're doing. If you have a question or want to share your story with others in future editions of this book, send me an email at Skamille@goldenleafpress.com

Good luck.

SJK

Jan 2011